The Dawn of the New Age

The Dawn of the New Age

Michael Green

daybreak
London

This edition published in 1993 by
Daybreak
Darton, Longman and Todd Ltd
1 Spencer Court
140–142 Wandsworth High Street
London SW18 4JJ

First published in 1982 as *The Day Death Died* by
Inter-Varsity Press
38 De Montfort Street, Leicester LE1 7GP

ISBN–0–232–51980–3

A catalogue record of this book is available from the British Library

Cover design: Leigh Hurlock

Phototypeset by Intype, London
Printed and bound in Great Britain by Page Bros, Norwich

For Jenny

Contents

Is it True . . . and Does it Matter?

Christianity is unique among the religions of the world. It is based on the conviction that its founder, Jesus Christ, rose again from the dead on the first Easter day.

Millions of people believe that with all their hearts: I am one of them. Millions more regard it, if they think about it at all, as a pious fairy story: the sort of thing that brings a crumb of comfort when you stand by an open grave, but not seriously to be reckoned with as real. Millions more have never really thought about it: it has never occurred to them to do so.

I have written this book for all three categories. I want Christians to have a clearer view of the resurrection of Jesus Christ, because its impact can transform every aspect of life. I want those with a vague faith, such as for years I had, to see the reality of the resurrection and come face to face with its dynamic power. And I want those who have never really looked into it to realize the solid basis, both in history and experience, for the resurrection of Jesus Christ: indeed, I want them to discover him personally.

It is perhaps a good thing – and certainly a convenient thing – that the crux of Christianity lies fairly and squarely in this single issue of the resurrection of Christ. It enables us to concentrate on a comparatively small door, but one which could open into a vast room. If Christ rose from the dead, then the implications are enormous. If he did not, then Christianity can be relegated to one of the mystery religions.

The resurrection is the cornerstone on which the whole of Christianity, both in its corporate and individual aspects, is built. If it is false, the entire edifice collapses. If it is true, the consequences for our world and for our individual lives are immense. That is why I have written this book. We live in a day when there is a new quest for spirituality, as is clear from the growth of the New Age. I salute the New Agers for their rejection of the shackles of materialism which have cramped the human spirit for so long. But I cannot commend them for their relapse into pantheism, the oldest delusion of mankind, and the irrationalism which is characteristic of the movement. No, the New Age dawned when Jesus rose from the dead. The first Easter is no myth: it happened. Resurrection is no vague hope for the Age of Aquarius: it has been a present reality ever since the powerfully attested resurrection of Jesus from the chill of death in the spring of AD 30.

If we want to pierce into the heart of the mystery of life, if we want to discover what human existence and destiny are all about, there is one place, and one only, to start. Did Jesus of Nazareth (on any showing the greatest of men) rise to a new life after three days of death, or did he not? Examine that event, for which the evidence is laid out in the pages that follow. Listen to the claims of Christian disciples that they not only know *about* this Jesus but have *met* him and share their lives with him. Then make up your own mind. People continue to ask two questions of the resurrection of Jesus: 'Is it true?' and 'Does it matter?' This book is intended to help us grapple with them. There is no more important quest in all the world.

Michael Green
Lambeth, 1992

1

The Heart of the Matter

What is life all about?

What is happening to our society, indeed to our world, as it seems to rush towards the brink of disaster, apparently out of control?

Is there a life beyond the grave? Or do we go out like a light?

Who has not asked such questions from time to time, before brushing them under the carpet because they are too uncomfortable? But trying to forget them does no good. They refuse to go away.

All the great religions of the world attempt an answer, however tentative, to issues like these. Christianity certainly does: and Christianity is the faith which, above all others, has affected the lives of millions of every colour, nationality and social class in the world over nearly two thousand years. It can make a very fair claim to universal appeal and relevance. But what lies at the heart of Christianity?

Is it primarily a matter of belief? Is it a pattern of Sunday church-going? Is it a code of conduct which tries to embody love? Or is it, maybe, just a widely diffused addition to the culture of the West?

Christianity is none of these things. Of course, Christians do have specific beliefs. They worship God together. They behave in a certain way. And to a greater or lesser extent they affect the climate of the society

in. But these things do not bring us to the
e matter.

to Christianity is the resurrection of Jesus
m the grave. That is the heart of the matter.
For Christianity does not claim that Jesus was a good
teacher and a fine man. It maintains that in Jesus God
broke into our world. His whole life was a demonstration of what God is like. And when men had crucified him through envy and hatred on the first Good
Friday, God raised him from the dead on Easter day,
thus vindicating his claims and his teaching, his life
and his sacrificial death.

That is, and always has been, the Christian claim. So
if you want to examine the truth of Christianity, and
whether or not you can credit the answers it gives to
the problems of our world, it is to the resurrection you
should turn.

Professor C. E. M. Joad, a former broadcaster and
philosopher at London University, was once asked
whom of all past figures in history he would most like
to meet, and what he would most like to ask him. He
replied that he would most like to meet Jesus Christ,
and he would want to ask him 'the most important
question in the world: "Did you or did you not rise
from the dead?" '.

There was one spot on the battlefield of Waterloo
which was taken and retaken three times during that
memorable day. Both Napoleon and Wellington saw its
vital importance and concentrated their attention upon
it. Its final capture by the British troops contributed in
large measure to the outcome of the battle. So it is with
the resurrection of Jesus Christ. Its significance is crucial
for believers and for enquirers alike. The resurrection
is essential for Christianity.

This was realized by two young students, West and
Lyttleton, in the cynical, pleasure-seeking days of the
eighteenth century, when unbelief was as fashionable
as it is today. They were friends of Dr Johnson and the

poet Alexander Pope. They were in the swim of soc
And they decided to attack Christianity at its very
So Lyttleton settled down to disprove the conversion
of Saul of Tarsus to Christianity, and West to prove
that Jesus never rose from the dead. When next they
met both were somewhat shamefaced. Each had a confession to make. In their study of the evidence they had
been forced to unwelcome conclusions. In Lyttleton's
case, he had found irrefutable evidence to show that
Saul, the famous persecutor of Christians, *had* turned
into Paul, the most celebrated missionary the Christian
church has ever had. And West had become convinced
that Jesus *did* rise from the dead. His book, *Observations
on the History and Evidences of the Resurrection of Jesus
Christ*, 1747, bears on its flyleaf the significant admon-
ition, 'Blame not before thou hast examined the truth.'

In our own day, a young journalist was inclined
towards the negative conclusions of sceptical theologians. He admired the character of Jesus, but felt his
story rested on insecure historical foundations, and that
the gospel materials were unreliable and late. He was
convinced that miracles do not happen now and did
not happen then. But the story of Jesus fascinated him.
He determined that when he had time he would look
into the matter, and write a sensitive and credible
account of those last tragic days of Jesus, the final phase
of a memorable life. But when he came to study the
evidence, he, like Gilbert West, was constrained to
write his book on the other side. Frank Morison's *Who
Moved the Stone?* has had a phenomenal popularity and
influence. With great honesty he has entitled the first
chapter 'The book which refused to be written'.

The evidence for the resurrection of Jesus Christ is
very strong. I invite you to come with me and examine
some of it. For without a doubt it is the lynchpin of
Christianity. It is the clearest clue we have to the purpose and destiny of life. It *is* the heart of the matter.

Central though it is, the resurrection is a subject that

is curiously avoided by many who call themselves Christians. Lord Ismay records that, when he was Chairman of the B.B.C., only one of the 6,000 sermons preached on the air had shed any light on this subject. And I remember visiting a consultant in a London hospital. He was lying in bed, dying of leukaemia. A specialist in the disease, he had developed it himself. I was called to see him. And he was angry. Not because of his disease, though he was only in his forties. But because of church leaders who speak in such muffled tones about the heart of Christianity. An agnostic for years he had, lying there in bed, read two books which had brought him to a clear and joyful faith in the risen Christ. And he asked, 'Why have I never had the evidence clearly put to me before?'

Consider the issues which hang on the resurrection of Jesus Christ.

If it is true, then we can be sure that God exists. And he is at once seen to be the sort of God that Jesus proclaimed him to be: one who not only made us but loves us, and cares for us so much that he came to be one of us.

If it is true, then there is a life after death. Jesus, who told us that in his Father's house were many resting-places, can be believed. He came back from death and demonstrated the truth of what he had taught.

If it is true, then Jesus Christ really is the Way, the Truth, the Life. No other religion has been able to make, let alone substantiate, a claim that its founder rose from the dead and is alive today. Jesus has every right to be considered *the* bridge between God and man – if he rose from the dead.

If it is true, then there is a future for mankind. His resurrection is a first instalment of the better world we all want but seem incapable of producing. But as the West German leader, Chancellor Adenauer, put it, 'If

Jesus Christ is not alive, I see no hope for the human race.'

If it is true, it puts suffering and death in a new light. It tells us that this life with all its pain and anguish is not the end: on the contrary, this life is a training-school for eternity. The first Easter was the day death died. Those who know the risen Christ will spend eternity with him. He who came to share our precarious life, offers us a share of his eternal life – *if* the resurrection story is true.

Yes, a great deal hangs on whether or not Jesus Christ rose from the dead. This is a subject on which nobody can afford to be agnostic. The stakes are too high. Mercifully, as Lord Darling, formerly Lord Chief Justice of England, once put it, 'We, as Christians, are asked to take a very great deal on trust: the teachings, for example, and the miracles of Jesus. If we had to take all on trust, I, for one, should be sceptical. The crux of the problem of whether Jesus was or was not what he proclaimed himself to be, must surely depend on the truth or otherwise of the resurrection. On that greatest point we are not merely asked to have faith. In its favour as a living truth there exists such overwhelming evidence, positive and negative, factual and circumstantial, that no intelligent jury in the world could fail to bring in the verdict that the resurrection story is true.'

The judge was certainly right in seeing the resurrection as the hinge on which the whole world of Christianity turned. Was he right in concluding that, incredible though it may seem, it actually happened? That is the question to which we turn in the chapters that follow.

2

Clearing the Ground

The proper way to approach any supposed event in the past is first of all to lay aside prejudice, secondly to hear the claim, thirdly to assess the evidence on which it rests, and fourthly to examine the presuppositions of those who make it. So let us follow those four steps as we begin to examine the resurrection of Jesus Christ.

Renounce prejudice
First, then, let us try to lay aside prejudice either in favour of the Christian claim or against it.

We are all influenced more than we care to admit by our background, the opinions of our friends, and the assumptions of our culture. Christians have no interest in obscurantism: after all, they follow one whom they claim to be the Truth. If Jesus did not rise from the dead, the sooner Christians stop maintaining he did, the better. There is no excuse for hiding behind tradition or for taking refuge in fairy tales because they are pleasant. If the resurrection is false, we should abandon the Christian camp for the humanist.

But there is a lot less of that thoughtless Christian prejudice around than there used to be. It is perhaps more common to find prejudice among those who, for one reason or another, have ignored or rejected the Christian claim.

A great many people could not care less. They say, 'Well, maybe he did rise from the dead; maybe he didn't. What does it matter?' This apathy, this indifference to truth, seems unfortunately to be on the increase in our society. Perhaps television has something to do with it. We cannot do much to affect the things we see on the screen: so why bother?

Whatever the cause, apathy is totally misguided, and it rests upon a misunderstanding. It is misguided because, as we saw at the end of the last chapter, the resurrection, if true, has the most staggering implications for every single person on this planet, and for the destiny of mankind as a whole. And the misunderstanding would seem to be that Jesus was just a man like the rest of us, and if he rose from the grave it is rather as if someone who had drowned was resuscitated by a kiss of life on Brighton beach. Of course, the Christian claim is nothing remotely like this. It is that Jesus Christ 'being raised from the dead will never die again: death no longer has dominion over him' (Romans 6:9). We are not talking about temporary resuscitation, but resurrection to a new and lasting quality of life.

If it is true, it is exceedingly important. So let us lay apathy aside, and see where the evidence leads us.

Theology, somewhat surprisingly, is also sometimes affected by prejudice. A great deal of modern theology is concerned to 'demythologize' (which often turns out to mean 'explain away') biblical concepts like the incarnation or the resurrection of Jesus. We must not, they say, present the Christian faith in such a way that makes it hard for people to believe. We must not stick to a literal, bodily resurrection. On the contrary, let us concede that the body of Jesus is rotting in some Palestinian grave, but that his spirit (whatever that may mean) lives on. We shall be examining this view in more depth later. Here it is sufficient to notice that it goes back to the eighteenth-century philosopher and theologian Schleiermacher, who wanted to preserve religion from the chill winds of science on the one hand and history on the other. But it is very hard to persuade the man in the street that such a procedure is not dishonest. Did Jesus rise or did he not? That remains the question: and it should certainly be open to the keenest critique of science and historical investigation.

A rather more subtle variety of the same theological prejudice is to be seen in the writings of Rudolf Bultmann and his followers. In deference to the existentialist philosophy prevailing on the continent for much of this century, Bultmann and his colleagues have argued that it is improper to seek to examine 'the Easter event'. We are not able to get back beyond 'the Easter faith'. The empty tomb, he rightly maintains, is not nearly so important as the risen presence of Christ. So he abandons faith in the physical resurrection of Jesus, locates his Christian confidence in the confession of the Easter faith by the early church, and construes it as meaning that the cross, which he believes to have been the end of the Jesus story, has saving significance.

Now there are all sorts of influences which have combined to lead Professor Bultmann to write as he does. We are not concerned with them at present. But three questions nevertheless force us to confront the position he has advanced. First, granted the importance of the Easter faith, what was the Easter fact which gave rise to it? Secondly, if Jesus did not rise from the dead, what sort of sense does it make to say that you have faith in him as living Lord? Thirdly, if history disproves Christianity, then Christianity is false, and it is much better to say so. A number of Bultmann's close disciples have in fact taken this step. Theological prejudice should not be allowed to keep us from examining the evidence of the New Testament. It is no good claiming that modern man will not credit the resurrection, or that its historicity is irrelevant once its symbolic force is granted. In sheer integrity, we must lay aside preconceptions and expose ourselves to the sources.

The third and most widespread form of prejudice on this subject springs from the study of science. The resurrection must be ruled out of court. It is impossible! Well, such dogmatism is not the normal way in which reputable scientists examine a problem. True, there is an impatience with miracles in many scientific circles, but it is matched by an increasing recognition of the limitations of our knowledge and the mystery of the universe.

There are just two points that need to be made with regard to science and the resurrection. The first concerns scientific method. This is unashamedly inductive. That is to say, it begins with the phenomena and then seeks to arrive at generalizations which account for them. It does not begin by ruling out of order facts which are inconvenient. Instead, it examines them. And most of the advances in scientific enquiry have taken place when scientists have wrestled with the one awkward fact which did not fit into the prevailing theory. In principle there is no scientific reason why Jesus could not have risen from the grave.

The second point that needs to be made is this: we are not claiming that there is a certain class of people that get up out of their coffins. The first-century writers weren't claiming this either.

What we are maintaining is that Jesus was no ordinary man. We believe that in this very special person, one who was more than man, the forces of death met their match. We believe that there are good reasons for supposing that Jesus was no less God than man. How then can we be sure that he could not overcome death? He lived a uniquely unsullied life, perfect at every point. How can we be certain that a life which had given no foothold to sin could not master death? We have no other example of the 'sinless' category to compare him with. Jesus made the whole of his credibility rest upon the assertion that he would 'do a Jonah' on his contemporaries; and just as Jonah came back from his three-day 'death' inside the great fish, so Jesus himself would come back from the jaws of death (Matthew 12:39–41).

So let us lay aside the dogmatic prejudice which asserts 'It could never happen' and see if, according to all the available evidence, it *did* happen in this one solitary case of Jesus. If he was perfect man, if he was more than man, we cannot rule it out of court.

Having attempted to recognize and divest ourselves of prejudice, let us hear the Christian claim about Jesus. Just what were his contemporaries laying claim to?

Hear the claim

First of all let us hear the earliest evidence in the New Testament, presented by Paul the apostle in the mid-fifties of the first century, just twenty years after the event:

> For I delivered to you as of first importance what I also received, that Christ died for our sins in accordance with the scriptures, that he was buried, that he was raised on the third day in accordance with the scriptures, and that he appeared to Cephas, then to the twelve. Then he appeared to more than five hundred brethren at one time, most of whom are still alive, though some have fallen asleep. Then he appeared to James, then to all the apostles. Last of all, as to one untimely born, he appeared also to me. For I am the least of the apostles, unfit to be called an apostle, because I persecuted the church of God. But by the grace of God I am what I am, and his grace toward me was not in vain . . . Whether then it was I or they, so we preach and so you believed.
>
> Now if Christ is preached as raised from the dead, how can some of you say that there is no resurrection of the dead? But if there is no resurrection of the dead, then Christ has not been raised; if Christ has not been raised, then our preaching is in vain and your faith is in vain. We are even found to be misrepresenting God, because we testified of

God that he raised Christ, whom he did not raise if it is true that the dead are not raised. For if the dead are not raised, then Christ has not been raised. If Christ has not been raised, your faith is futile and you are still in your sins. Then those also who have fallen asleep in Christ have perished. If for this life only we have hoped in Christ, we are of all men most to be pitied.

But in fact Christ has been raised from the dead, the first fruits of those who have fallen asleep.

1 Corinthians 15:3–20

The material Paul quotes is of the utmost value. It was probably written very soon after Jesus lived, and it shows how fundamental the resurrection was to Paul, to the Jerusalem apostles, and to the Christians in Corinth as well. It was clearly at the very heart of the faith.

Ten years later we find Peter taking up his pen and exclaiming,

Blessed be the God and Father of our Lord Jesus Christ! By his great mercy we have been born anew to a living hope through the resurrection of Jesus Christ from the dead, and to an inheritance which is imperishable, undefiled, and unfading, kept in heaven for you, who by God's power are guarded through faith for a salvation ready to be revealed in the last time.

1 Peter 1:3–5

Those to whom this letter was addressed were in imminent danger of a summary trial and agonizing death for their faith: hundreds of Christians were burnt alive in Nero's persecution of AD 64, a situation which may well be reflected in this letter. So Peter continues:

In this you rejoice, though now for a little while you may have to suffer various trials, so that the genuineness of your faith, more precious than gold which is perishable though tested by fire, may redound to praise and glory and honour

at the revelation of Jesus Christ. Without having seen him you love him; though you do not now see him you believe in him and rejoice with unutterable and exalted joy.

1 Peter 1:6–8

A few verses later he bursts out:

Through him you have confidence in God, who raised him from the dead and gave him glory, so that your faith and hope are in God.

1 Peter 1:21

There can be no doubt that the resurrection was of crucial importance for both the writer and the recipients of this letter.

The letter to Hebrew Christians was probably written about AD 68 and calls 'the resurrection of the dead' one of the 'elementary doctrines' of the Christian faith, so cardinal is it, and so universally believed in the Christian church. This remarkable letter concentrates our gaze on Jesus as the eternal high priest, reconciling man and God in a way in which no other priesthood has ever been able to do.

The former priests were many in number, because they were prevented by death from continuing in office; but he holds his priesthood permanently, because he continues for ever. Consequently he is able for all time to save those who draw near to God through him, since he always lives to make intercession for them.

Hebrews 7:23–25

Or again

When Christ had offered for all time a single sacrifice for sins, he sat down at the right hand of God, then to wait until his enemies should be made a stool for his feet.

Hebrews 10:12–13

Mark is usually considered the earliest of the Gospels, and it was probably written by the mid-sixties of the first century AD. Mark records three predictions by Jesus of what is going to befall him. They come in 8:31, 9:31 and 10:33–34. They all envisage a bloody, treacherous death for Jesus, and they all indicate that he will rise again on the third day. Mark's actual account of what took place at Easter is instructive:

> And when the sabbath was past, Mary Magdalene, and Mary the mother of James, and Salome, bought spices, so that they might go and anoint him. And very early on the first day of the week they went to the tomb when the sun had risen. And they were saying to one another, 'Who will roll away the stone for us from the door of the tomb?' And looking up, they saw that the stone was rolled back; for it was very large. And entering the tomb, they saw a young man sitting on the right side, dressed in a white robe; and they were amazed. And he said to them, 'Do not be amazed; you seek Jesus of Nazareth, who was crucified. He has risen, he is not here; see the place where they laid him. But go, tell his disciples and Peter that he is going before you to Galilee; there you will see him, as he told you.' And they went out and fled from the tomb; for trembling and astonishment had come upon them; and they said nothing to any one, for they were afraid.

Mark 16:1–8

With these remarkable words Mark's Gospel comes to an abrupt end. It may be he intended it to end there, with awe and amazement before the ultimate act of God in raising Christ from the grave. It may be that he was arrested or otherwise prevented from completing the Gospel. At all events, the original text finished there and in the second century three alternative versions competed for the honour of bringing the Gospel to an end!

It is widely held that Matthew's Gospel was written

in the eighties, while Luke's Gospel and the Acts of the Apostles are variously dated in the sixties or eighties. There is a great deal about the resurrection in all three.

Matthew tells us that as the women left the tomb with fear and great joy and ran to tell the disciples,

> *Jesus met them and said, 'Hail!' And they came up and took hold of his feet and worshipped him. Then Jesus said to them, 'Do not be afraid; go and tell my brethren to go to Galilee, and there they will see me. . . . Now the eleven disciples went to Galilee, to the mountain to which Jesus had directed them. And when they saw him they worshipped him; but some doubted. And Jesus came and said to them, 'All authority in heaven and on earth has been given to me. Go therefore and make disciples of all nations, baptizing them in the name of the Father and of the Son and of the Holy Spirit, teaching them to observe all that I have commanded you; and lo, I am with you always, to the close of the age.'*

Matthew 28:9–10, 16–20

With those words Matthew brings his Gospel to an end.

Luke's account is too long to quote here. It comes in chapter 24 of his Gospel and, after telling of the empty tomb and the women, goes on to recount the matchless story of two disciples, discouraged and fed up, walking to Emmaus on Easter afternoon. Jesus joins them: they do not recognize him until he excites them by explaining the scriptures to them, and reveals himself to them in the way he breaks bread at table. Amazed and thrilled, they return to Jerusalem by night, and find the disciples saying 'The Lord has risen indeed, and has appeared to Simon!' What happened at that interview with Simon, Luke does not record. But he does tell of various meetings of the risen Christ with his disciples, before he leaves them for the last time and returns to his Father in heaven.

The Acts of the Apostles are full of references to the resurrection. This book was written to take the story of Jesus into its second stage, as his disciples began to spread all over the ancient world the account of the amazing person they had been privileged to know, and the achievements of his life, death and resurrection. The resurrection and ascension of Jesus are summarized in the first paragraph of the book, and then one of the qualifications of replacement for the traitor Judas is laid down: he must be 'with us a witness to his resurrection' (Acts 1:22).

The whole of the rest of the book is concerned with the witness to the resurrection which was the prime differentiating mark of the early Christians: apart from that they were hardly distinguishable from other Jews. But they had the effrontery to maintain that Jesus, whom their rulers had condemned and whom the Romans had executed, was the Son of God, and that God had raised him from the tomb. This was insurrection indeed. So they were opposed, imprisoned, tortured and killed for the message which had brought their movement into being.

The story begins in Jerusalem with their forthright preaching on the Day of Pentecost:

Men of Israel, hear these words: Jesus of Nazareth, a man attested to you by God with mighty works and wonders and signs which God did through him in your midst, as you yourselves know – this Jesus, delivered up according to the definite plan and foreknowledge of God, you crucified and killed by the hands of lawless men. But God raised him up, having loosed the pangs of death, because it was not possible for him to be held by it . . . This Jesus God raised up, and of that we all are witnesses.

Acts 2:22–24, 32

There is a great deal more in this vein. Luke's summary of the spread of the gospel in that first Jerusalem community is as follows:

> *And with great power the apostles gave their testimony to the resurrection of the Lord Jesus, and great grace was upon them all.*
>
> Acts 4:33

Three other examples from the later parts of the book make the prime importance of the resurrection obvious. At Athens Paul so concentrated on *Iesous kai anastasis* (Jesus and resurrection) that they thought he was announcing a couple of new deities (Acts 17:18)! Again, Paul in prison and making his defence before the Roman governor, Felix, can say 'With respect to the resurrection of the dead I am on trial before you this day' (Acts 24:21). Once more he makes the issue abundantly plain in his trial before King Agrippa:

> *I stand here testifying both to small and great, saying nothing but what the prophets and Moses said would come to pass: that the Christ must suffer, and that, by being the first to rise from the dead, he would proclaim light both to the people and to the Gentiles.*
>
> Acts 26:22–23

Our survey of the New Testament evidence is almost complete. We ought, however, to glance at the Gospel of John and the Revelation of John, both of which were probably completed in the nineties of the first century. The Gospel tells how Jesus appeared to Mary Magdalene, to the twelve, to Thomas, and to Peter and John. It is a marvellous piece of writing. It breathes authenticity. Read the last two chapters of St John's Gospel for yourself and feel the force of them. Could they have been written by a mind deranged? Could they have been written to deceive? And notice that these two chapters do not come from the author of the Gospel in isolation. He speaks for the Christian community to which he belongs, and that community puts its hand to what he writes:

This is the disciple who is bearing witness to these things, and who has written these things; and we know *that his testimony is true.*

John 21:24

As for the book of Revelation, the whole theme hinges on the proposition that 'the Lamb once slain is in the midst of the throne of God'. It claims that in the death and resurrection of Jesus we have the clue to the meaning of history and the destiny of man. Because of the resurrection we can face the utmost in catastrophe confident that 'the Lord God omnipotent is reigning'. Nowhere does the basic claim come through more clearly than in 1:17–18 where John has a vision of the living Christ:

When I saw him, I fell at his feet as though dead. But he laid his right hand upon me, saying, 'Fear not, I am the first and the last, and the living one; I died, and behold I am alive for evermore, and I have the keys of Death and Hades.'

Assess the evidence
Such, in brief, is the evidence from the New Testament. How shall we assess it?

First, I am struck by the breadth of this testimony. It is brought before us in every strand of the material: Matthew, Mark, Luke, John, all have independent elements within them, derived from different eye-witnesses. The resurrection plays an equally important part in the writings of Peter and Paul, and in Hebrews and Revelation. If it is not true, then the whole of the New Testament would need to be rewritten.

Secondly, I am impressed by the harmony of this material. It is by no means copied from one writer by another. There are what appear to be minor discrepancies: thus Mark speaks of one young man (?angel) at the tomb, Luke of two. The writers are clearly struggling to describe the indescribable. They allude to the doubt which struck the disciples, before it turned into joy: they were not easy meat for a fraud.

Thirdly, the antiquity of this testimony is impressive. It is written between twenty and sixty years after the event, all the different strands of it. And that is very early by ancient reckoning.

Tacitus is the main Roman historian of the Empire in the time of Jesus. He wrote some eighty years after most of the events he described, yet his accuracy is rated very highly. The other major historian of this period, Suetonius, wrote a century after the events he described. Within Judaism itself, the First Book of Maccabees was written about 100 BC and tells of the exploits of the freedom fighters seventy years earlier. This does not prevent its being considered a most reliable document.

Why, then, should we discredit the Gospel records (when the gap between event and writing is much shorter, and the attestation much broader) simply because Jesus was not an ordinary person and the events of his life and death were not ordinary events?

The famous scientist, Ambrose Fleming, makes this point well:

We must ask ourselves whether it is probable that such a book, describing events that occurred about thirty or forty years previously, could have been accepted and cherished if the stories of abnormal events in it were false or mythical. It is impossible, because the memory of all elderly persons regarding the events of history thirty or forty years before is perfectly clear. No-one could now issue a biography of Queen Victoria, who died thirty-one years ago, full of anecdotes which were quite untrue. They would be contradicted at once. They would certainly not be generally accepted and passed on as true. Hence there is a great improbability that the account of the resurrection given by the Gospels is a pure invention. This mythical theory has had to be abandoned because it will not bear close scrutiny.

Is there any external support for the resurrection of Jesus Christ? There is, both in Roman and Jewish sources and perhaps in archaeology too.

Tacitus, describing the Fire of Rome in AD 64, tells how Christians were made scapegoats by the Emperor Nero for this blaze:

> The name Christian comes to them from Christ, who was executed in the reign of Tiberius by the procurator Pontius Pilate; and the pernicious superstition, suppressed for a while, broke out afresh and spread, not only through Judea, the source of the malady, but even throughout Rome itself, where everything vile is fêted.
>
> *Annals* 15.44

Tacitus was writing about AD 112, and at the same time Pliny, governor of Bithynia, was asking the Emperor Trajan what he should do about the growth of Christians in his area, whose monotheism was threatening the sale of sacrificial animals, the survival of the temples and the prestige of the emperor. He says that the Christians lived exemplary lives, but refused to worship the images of the gods. Rather, they met on a certain fixed day (*i.e.* Sunday, the day on which Christians claimed the resurrection took place) and sang in alternate verses a hymn 'to Christ as God' (*Epistles* 10.96).

Josephus, the Jewish general turned historian, wrote

about the turn of the century, and his work contains a remarkable passage about Jesus, worth quoting in full:

> And there arose about this time Jesus, a wise man, if indeed we should call him a man; for he was a doer of marvellous deeds, a teacher of men who receive the truth with pleasure. He won over many Jews and also many Greeks. This man was the Messiah. And when Pilate had condemned him to the cross at the instigation of our own leaders, those who had loved him did not at once cease. For he appeared to them the third day alive again, as the holy prophets had predicted, and said many other wonderful things about him. And even now the race of Christians, so called after him, has not yet died out.
>
> *Antiquities* 18.3.3

This remarkable passage has attracted a lot of attention. Many scholars cannot believe it was genuinely written by Josephus. There may be some Christian interpolation here, though it is hard to imagine Christians being so restrained! Moreover the manuscript tradition is uniform in attributing this passage to Josephus himself. Some of the paragraph is doubtless sarcastic: Josephus was no Christian. 'If indeed we should call him a man' may be an allusion to his divine claims, and 'this man was the Messiah' may refer to the charge affixed to his cross, while the passage about the resurrection may merely reflect Christian preaching. Nevertheless, we have here a remarkable independent testimony to the person, death, resurrection and continuing influence of Jesus among Jews at the end of the first century.

The archaeological evidence is, from the very nature of the case, incapable of being more than circumstantial. But it is intriguing all the same. It indicates that both the account of Jesus' death and rumours of his resurrection were known to the Roman authorities very early indeed, and that they took swift remedial action.

A remarkable inscription has turned up, belonging to the reign of either Tiberius (AD 14–38) or Claudius (AD 41–54). In it the emperor expresses his displeasure at reports he has heard of the removal of dead bodies from the tomb, and he warns that he will punish, by the unusual expedient of the death penalty, any further tampering with graves. This inscription was found in Nazareth, the birthplace of Jesus. Pilate must have reported about Jesus to the emperor in Rome: as a matter of fact, Tertullian, a Christian lawyer in the second century, claimed that Pilate's report was still extant in the imperial archives. Presumably Pilate would have taken the line (alluded to in Matthew 28:11ff.) that the disciples came and stole the body of Jesus while the soldiers who were supposed to be guarding the tomb had fallen asleep. This would be quite enough to account for the sharp imperial rejoinder!

Examine the presuppositions

Such is the attestation for the resurrection of Jesus from a whole breadth of Christian sources, together with Roman, Jewish and archaeological support. What are we to make of this evidence? What were the expectations of those first Christians?

Is it simply a case of their being poor, uncritical folk, unable to tell a ghost or a vision from a resurrected friend? I think not. Resurrections were no more common in the first century than they are now. The first disciples were no mere simpletons, easily taken in. Had they been, they would have made few converts in the sophisticated society of the Graeco-Roman world, and fewer still among their fellow Jews.

Were they, then, wicked deceivers, determined to get

a following for themselves? That is equally incredible.
For one thing you do not allow yourself to be torn limb
from limb for a fraud. Had the early Christians been
deceivers, some at least of them would have given way
under torture.

Moreover they would not have left so many loose
ends in their story. It is no easier to harmonize all the
details of the resurrection accounts than it is to reconcile
accounts of the same event in eight different news-
papers. But had the early Christians been making it all
up they would have made sure that their stories tallied.
They would have ensured that the appearances were
either all of a spiritual Jesus or of a resuscitated, tangible
Jesus, not a curious mixture of the two. No, the artless
lack of collusion, the absence of contrived agreement
in these stories militates against their being fabrication.
These stories were not made up.

Very well then, were the early Christians resorting to
wish-fulfilment? Were they so anxious to see the resurrection of their friend and master that they came to
believe it had happened?

The trouble with such a view is that there is no evidence whatever to support it. On the contrary, the
accounts indicate that the disciples had no expectation
that Jesus would return from the grave. He had said
he would, but frankly, they did not believe him. When
they were confronted by the events of Easter day, they
were dumbfounded, and at first refused to believe it.

And as for the preposterous notion, presented by some
theologians (who should know better), that they made
it all up from a random collection of Old Testament
texts and expectations, this is even further from the
mark. As Jews they certainly looked for resurrection. It
had been *implicit* in their faith from the days of Abraham onwards. Did not God reveal himself, saying 'I am
(not *I was*) the God of Abraham, Isaac and Jacob'? This

faith in the resurrection had been *explicit* at least since the book of Daniel was written (Daniel 12:2). But it was always associated with the end time, the climax of history. Martha, the woman whose brother, Lazarus, Jesus was about to resuscitate, expressed Jewish orthodoxy precisely in her reply to Jesus. 'Your brother will rise again', Jesus had said. Martha said to him, 'I know that he will rise again in the resurrection *at the last day*' (John 11:23–24).

No, the disciples had no expectation that Jesus would rise from the dead before that last day, and they certainly did not dream up his resurrection out of texts from the Old Testament. There are remarkably few such texts, and they all refer to the final resurrection of the just at the end of the world, not to God's vindication of his Messiah in their own lifetime.

One more question before we turn, in the next chapter, to examine the evidence which persuaded these Jews that their Jesus was alive again, and for ever.

Can we reconcile their testimony to the risen Jesus with a purely spiritual resurrection? Could they have meant that the body of Jesus stayed in the tomb but that his spirit lived on – a sort of 'John Brown's body lies a-mouldering in the grave, but his soul goes marching on'? Once again, the answer must be negative, and that for a variety of reasons.

In the first place it is very hard to see what is meant by a spiritual resurrection. How would you know if you met one? How would it be different from happy memories of the departed or his continuing influence?

Secondly, a spiritual resurrection would make nonsense of the claim explicitly referred to in most of the accounts we have looked at, that the resurrection took place *on the third day*.

Thirdly, it would leave untouched the problem of what happened to the corpse, or why the tomb never became a place of pilgrimage.

Fourthly, a spiritual resurrection in AD 30 is totally at odds with the convictions of Judaism that people would have a physical resurrection at the last day. Wherever resurrection is referred to in Judaism, there is a firm belief in the *resurrection of the body*. This comes both in Old Testament passages like Ezekiel 37, and in the Jewish writings which came after the Old Testament was complete, such as Judith 16:17, 2 Baruch 49:2–50:4, Sibylline Oracles 4.179–182. Physical resurrection was the unvarying hope of the Jews. The Pharisees held it especially strongly. It is incredible that the disciples would have been trained in any other view. Moreover, as we have seen in 1 Corinthians 15, Paul is at pains to show that Jesus was *buried*, and that it was as one dead and buried that he rose again on the third day (15:4). The whole thrust of this chapter is directed not against materialists who thought that this life was all there is, but against Greeks who believed in the immortality of the soul. Paul does not say to them 'Right, have it your way. Resurrection is just my way of talking about the immortality of the soul, which you believe.' He roundly tells them that if they do not believe in the resurrection of Jesus their faith is vain, their salvation is at risk, their dead are lost, and they are of all men most to be pitied.

We may safely conclude, therefore, that the early Christians were not simpletons or deceivers, that they were not indulging in fantasies of wish-fulfilment or extrapolations from obscure Old Testament texts. They were not maintaining the doctrine of the immortality of the soul.

They were making a claim utterly unique in the history of the world. They were saying that in Jesus the forces of death had met their match. Easter was, in a profound sense, the dawn of the new age. The grave had not been able to hold the prince of life. In the next chapter we shall need to look more closely at the evidence for this most remarkable of claims, which marks out Christianity from every other faith in the world.

3

Examining the Evidence

There is good evidence for the resurrection of Jesus Christ from the dead. 'It is not too much to say', wrote Bishop Westcott, one of the greatest New Testament scholars England has ever produced, 'that there is no single historical incident better or more variously attested than the resurrection of Christ.' And Sir Edward Clarke, a High Court judge, gives an interesting perspective on the matter when he writes:

> As a laywer I have made a prolonged study of the evidence for the events of Easter Day. To me the evidence is conclusive, and over and over again in the High Court I have secured the verdict on evidence not nearly so compelling. As a lawyer I accept the Gospel evidence unreservedly as the testimony of truthful men to facts that they were able to substantiate.

Or take Thomas Arnold, headmaster of Rugby, who was once Professor of History at Oxford. He put it like this:

> I have been used for many years to study the history of other times, and to examine and weigh the evidence of those who have written about them; and I know of no fact in the history of mankind which is proved by better and fuller evidence of every sort, to

the understanding of a fair inquirer, than the great sign that God has given us, that Christ died and rose again from the dead.

These three men, a lawyer, a secular historian and a New Testament scholar, agree that the evidence for the resurrection is overwhelming. What brought them to this conclusion?

The judicial murder of Jesus of Nazareth is not a pleasant story. He was done to death with the connivance of the religious and secular authorities and the backing of public opinion. After a sleepless night, in which he was given no food, endured the mockery of two trials, and had his back lacerated with the cruel Roman cat-o'-nine-tails, he was crucified – an excruciatingly painful death in which every nerve in the body screamed with anguish.

Jesus was dead
He died in an unusually quick time, six hours or so. The four executioners came to examine him before a friend, Joseph of Arimathea, was allowed to take away the body for burial.

These soldiers were experienced at their grisly task: crucifixions were not uncommon in Palestine. They knew a dead man when they saw one – and their commanding officer had heard the condemned man's death-cry himself, and was prepared to certify the death to the governor, Pontius Pilate. But just to make doubly sure, they pierced his heart through with a spear. And then a very remarkable thing happened.

We are told on eyewitness authority that 'blood and water' came out of the pierced side of Jesus (John 19:34–35). The eyewitness clearly attached great importance to this. Had Jesus still been alive when the spear pierced his side, strong spurts of blood would have emerged with every heartbeat. Instead, the observer noticed semi-solid dark red clots seeping out, distinct and separate from the accompanying watery serum. This is evidence of massive clotting of the blood in the main arteries, and is exceptionally strong medical proof of death. It is all the more impressive because the evangelist could not possibly have realized its significance to a pathologist.

The 'blood and water' from the spear-thrust is proof positive that Jesus was already dead.

Jesus was buried

After his death was certified, Jesus was taken down from the cross and buried in a rock tomb nearby, belonging to a hitherto secret disciple, Joseph of Arimathea. The body was placed on a stone ledge, wound tightly in strips of cloth, and covered with spices. John's Gospel tells us some seventy-five pounds were used, and that is likely enough. Joseph was a rich man, and no doubt wanted to make up for his cowardice during the lifetime of Jesus by giving him a splendid burial. The amount, though great, has parallels. Rabbi Gamaliel, a contemporary of Jesus, was buried with eighty pounds of spice when he died.

But details like this make nonsense of the theory that Jesus was not really dead, and that, revived in the cool of the tomb, he crept out and persuaded his gullible disciples that he was risen from the dead.

This rationalistic refuge from the strong evidence for the resurrection has a long ancestry. It was produced by Schleiermacher in 1799 and was revived in the 1960s by Hugh Schonfield in *The Passover Plot*. It ignores the deadly character of Jesus' wounds, the careful examination by experienced Roman executioners, the blood and water, the constricting grave-clothes, the crushing weight of spices, the lack of human help, and the sealed tomb.

What is more, it is psychologically impossible. How could someone who crept half dead out of a tomb, needing bandaging, strengthening, and every care, have persuaded his followers that he was the Lord of life and conqueror of death?

Granted, then, the death and burial of Jesus, what solid grounds are there for supposing that he rose from the dead?

1.   THE EMPTY TOMB

As we have seen in the records we looked at in the last chapter, the women who came to pay their last respects to Jesus on the first Easter morning by anointing his body (omitted in the haste of his burial before sundown on Friday) were shattered to find that his body had gone.

It is difficult to deny that the tomb of Jesus was empty on the first Easter day – unless we resort to the historical oddity, suggested by Kirsopp Lake, that they went to the wrong tomb! Did Joseph not know his own tomb? Would the authorities not speedily have exhumed Jesus, if his body had been there to find? Would the whole Christian movement have got under way on the basis of a wrong identification of tombs in the half-light of Easter morning? No, scepticism must do better than that if it is to win adherents.

The tomb was empty, and this was common ground between friend and foe alike. What the Jews did was not to deny that the tomb was empty, but to offer a natural explanation for the fact. 'The disciples of Jesus', they said, 'have stolen his body out of the tomb' (Matthew 28:12–15). Could the fact that the tomb was empty have any more certain confirmation than that?

It is sometimes said that our earliest witness, Paul, writing twenty years after the event, knows nothing of the empty tomb. His testimony is certainly of the utmost importance. If he knew nothing of the empty tomb we might have to be rather cautious in asserting it. But glance back at his words which were quoted on page 10. Does it seem to you that he is talking about a vague spiritual survival rather than something palpable and dateable: a resurrection?

1 Corinthians 15 is a truly remarkable piece of writing. It comes from one who had been a chief opponent of the Christian cause – until he was himself turned round in mid-career by the resurrection. The message of the resurrection which he stresses in this passage is something he considers 'as of first importance'. It is the very heart of Christianity.

Notice that he is not informing the Corinthians of something they did not know, but reminding them of something they heard and accepted at their conversion. That tradition (for such is the meaning, both in Hebrew and Greek, of 'I delivered to you', 'I received') derives from the very people who had been there, the Jerusalem Christians (see verse 11). He particularly singles out Peter (with his old Aramaic name, 'Cephas', in verse 5) and James (the brother of Jesus, who was converted through the resurrection, verse 7).

Not only does the tradition Paul refers to in this passage come from the central core of earliest believers, but it goes back to within a few years of the resurrection itself. Paul says that he 'received' this message (verse 3). When? Naturally, at his conversion on the Damascus Road, confirmed by subsequent discussions with the Jerusalem leadership. Paul could not have been converted later than AD 35. So what he gives us here is bedrock Christian belief which was already 'tradition' in Christian circles by the time Paul became a Christian, a few years after the events themselves! It is impossible to exaggerate the importance of 1 Corinthians 15.

Does it know anything of the empty tomb?

To be sure, Paul does not explicitly mention the empty tomb here. After all, he is not informing them, but reminding them! But he certainly knew it, and there are various allusions to it in this passage.

First, he says Jesus was raised *on the third day*. What does that mean? Surely (as in Acts 10:40), that on the third day the tomb of Jesus was found to be empty and Jesus was found to be alive.

Secondly, what would have been the point of saying 'he was buried . . . he was raised' (verse 4) unless Paul was alluding to the empty tomb? He is asserting that Jesus was raised from burial.

Thirdly, he makes considerable play in this chapter with the parallel between Christ's resurrection body and the body God will give to Christians in the resurrection (verses 12ff., 16, 20–23, 35–49). We know from his second letter to the Christians in Corinth that Paul did not think of our resurrection in non-bodily terms (2 Corinthians 5:1–4), which means that he did not think of Christ's resurrection in non-bodily terms either. He maintains that just as the physical body of Jesus was transformed at his resurrection, so it will be with the Christians at the last day. This sort of analogy would have been utterly impossible for Paul had he not believed that the body of Jesus was raised from death. The very way he spoke about *the body* in resurrection shows that he knew about the empty tomb.

And remember that 'resurrection' *meant* bodily resurrection to Paul, like any other Pharisee. You can search the rabbinic writings in vain to find any mention of a 'spiritual resurrection'. Often, indeed, they spoke of it in terms so crass that the New Testament writers have to protest against this element in their background and speak of a 'spiritual body'. But a body it remains.

There can be no doubt, then, that Paul knew the tradition of the empty tomb, and accepted it without bothering to discuss it at length. Like the other Christians, he was much more interested in the risen Jesus than in his empty tomb. Professor Sir Norman Anderson makes this point in an interesting and acute way:

Have you noticed that the references to the empty tomb all come in the Gospels which were written to give the Christian community the facts they wanted to know? In the public preaching to those who were not believers, as recorded in the Acts of the Apostles, there is an enormous emphasis on the fact of the resurrection but not a single reference to the empty tomb. Now, why? To me there is only one answer. There was no point in arguing about the empty tomb. Everyone, friend and opponent, knew that it was empty. The only questions worth arguing about were why it was empty and what its emptiness proved.

Well, what did its emptiness prove? And why was it empty that first Easter day? Supposing the body of Jesus was not raised by God, but removed by men, who would have wanted to do such a thing? There are only two lots of people to consider: his enemies, who crucified him, or his friends, who loved him. Nobody else. The trouble is that neither of these two parties were in the least likely to have done anything of the sort.

The disciples are the most obvious suspects. But the longer you think about it the less plausible it seems. And for two reasons. They could not have done it if they had wanted to. And they would not have done it if they had been able to.

They could not have removed the body of Jesus, for the simple reason that there was a guard on the tomb. It is fashionable to disregard the account of the guard, on the grounds that it is recorded only in Matthew's Gospel, and in any case looks like Christian propaganda. To my mind, however, it rings true. It is attested, incidentally, by two of the apocryphal Gospels of the second century, and by intelligent Christian writers like the philosopher Justin and the lawyer Tertullian, also in the second century. Furthermore it is just what you might expect to happen, given the mixture of

law and intrigue that went to make up the adminis-
tration of the province of Judea.

The body of a condemned criminal remained Roman
property. That is why Joseph had to go and ask no less
a person than the governor for it. As soon as Pilate said
'Yes' the whole situation changed. The body was now
back in Jewish custody. Responsibility for any riots that
might ensue would fall fairly and squarely upon Jewish
shoulders.

That is what made the chief priests pluck up courage
to brave the governor again, although they knew he
was in a black mood, in order to try to persuade him
to furnish them with a guard. They were playing the
age-old game of passing the buck. But Pilate refused to
be drawn. 'You have a guard of soldiers; go, make it as
secure as you can' (Matthew 27:65). They had indeed:
the temple police. Their plan to evade responsibility
had failed. Ruefully they set their own guard, having
failed to get his! But this did not prevent the tomb being
empty on the third day.

So afterwards the priests had to produce the lame
story of the watchmen sleeping on duty while the
Christians made off with the corpse. Not very good for
morale, but better than admitting the resurrection!

How anyone could suppose this story arose in Christian circles for apologetic reasons has always amazed
me. The resurrection of Jesus needed no such bolstering
to these early disciples. They were far too sure of the
reality of the risen Lord in their midst to go round
inventing stories of how his tomb came to be empty.

In any case, there are two tell-tale words in the
account which settle the matter – *hēmōn koimōmenōn*,
'while we slept' (Matthew 28:13). No Christian could
have made that up and put it in the mouth of the
guards. For if the guards had been sleeping, how could
they have known what the Christians were up to? No,
the story would only have been of use in Christian
propaganda *if the guards had stayed awake!*

The only conceivable reason, therefore, for the circulation of the story about a guard being set on the tomb was that it was true. There had been a guard. It had not prevented the resurrection. And it is eminently credible that the guard was bribed by the Jewish authorities to say that the disciples came and stole the body while they slept. The authorities were simply making the best of a bad situation. All in all, the guard on the sealed tomb, complete with a massive millstone at the door, make it very difficult to suppose that the friends of Jesus could possibly have removed the corpse.

And anyway, would they have wanted to? All the records show that they did not expect Jesus to rise from the dead. They were utterly disheartened. They had backed a loser, and all they wanted to do was to run away and hide and forget all about the fiasco. Resurrection seems never to have entered their heads.

But even if it were possible to credit these eleven men with such cunning at the moment of their greatest humiliation, what are we to make of the sequel? They were soon joyfully proclaiming the resurrection all over the world, and nothing could stop them. Prison, torture and death proved totally inadequate to change their conviction that Jesus was alive. No, the theory that the disciples stole the body of Jesus is psychologically untenable. They could not if they would, and they would not if they could.

It is no less incredible that the enemies of Jesus removed his body. At long last they had got him where they wanted him. Let him stay there! Would the chief priests, who went to all the trouble of organizing a guard over the tomb, have been so incredibly stupid as to suggest the idea of the resurrection by removing the body? And if, by some quirk of illogicality, they had been so stupid, they would have had no problem in producing the body once the disciples started preaching the resurrection – less than six weeks after the execution! Instead, all they could do was to order the Christians to be silent, and imprison or execute them when they refused to. No, we can be absolutely sure that the enemies of Jesus did not remove his corpse from the tomb. That is a possibility we can rule out.

Before we leave the question of the tomb, spare a thought for the grave-clothes. We are told that the grave-clothes were left behind in the tomb. One wonders why, if the body was pilfered by friend or enemy. But there is more to it than this. There is an eyewitness account, contained in John's Gospel, which says of Peter and John: 'Simon Peter came, following him, and went into the tomb; he saw the linen cloths lying, and the napkin, which had been on his head, not lying with the linen cloths but rolled up in a place by itself . . . and he (John) saw and believed' (John 20:6–8).

Why should this fact have made such an impression on John? For this reason. The wrappings were like a chrysalis case when the butterfly has emerged: undisturbed, but empty. Those tightly-wound bandages had encased Jesus as closely as the chrysalis case fits round the pupa. The turban round his head would, of course, have been separate from the wrappings round his body: that too was empty. But like the grave-clothes, it retained the shape it had when twirled round the head of Jesus.

That is what made such a profound impression on John. It almost seemed as though the body of Jesus had vaporized and had passed through the grave-clothes. Those which had covered his body were intact, apart from the fact that they were crushed by the weight of spices now there was no body inside. The turban kept its original shape.

What could account for such a strange phenomenon? No grave-robber would have been able to enact so remarkable a thing. He would simply have taken the body, grave-clothes and all. Had Jesus merely been resuscitated, he would presumably either have used the clothes or laid them aside. But as it was, all the signs point to Jesus' having been raised to a new order of life, a new sphere of existence. And he left the grave-clothes behind as the butterfly emerging to a new dimension of life leaves behind the cocoon. That sight convinced Peter and John. How about you?

2. THE RESURRECTION APPEARANCES

The empty tomb alone would never have brought about widespread belief in the resurrection. It would have occasioned only bewilderment. But something happened on that Sunday which explained why the tomb was found empty, and it sent the friends of Jesus into the streets with joy on their faces and courage in their hearts to proclaim that death had been unable to chain him.

This 'something' was the appearance of Jesus, alive, to some of his friends, on the first Easter day. During the six weeks that followed there were many such meetings. The Gospels profess to give us only a selection of events in the story of Jesus (John 21:25), but even so there is an impressive catalogue.

He appeared to Mary Magdalene (Mark 16:9; John 20:1–18), to the women (Matthew 28:1–10), to Simon Peter (Luke 24:34; 1 Corinthians 15:5), to the disciples on the road to Emmaus (Luke 24:13–31), to the eleven, and other disciples (Matthew 28:16–20; Luke 24:36–49; John 20:19–23; 21:1–14; Acts 1:3–9; 1 Corinthians 15:5–6), to Thomas (John 20:24–29), to James (1 Corinthians 15:7), to Joseph and Matthias (Acts 1:22–23), to five hundred people at once (1 Corinthians 15:6), to Peter and John (John 21:15–24) and to Paul (Acts 9:4ff.; 1 Corinthians 9:1; 15:8).

Together these appearances to individuals and to groups, to men and to women, in country and in town, in the upper room and by the open lake, constitute testimony to the resurrection that has to be taken very seriously indeed.

Why, it might be asked, does Paul not refer in his catalogue in 1 Corinthians 15 to the appearances of Jesus to the women? Answer: because he is summarizing the Jerusalem gospel tradition which he is passing on. And the Jerusalem gospel, proclaimed to Jews, would not have made use of testimony by women. One of the oldest commentaries on the Law of Moses states that evidence is not normally acceptable from a woman (Siphre on Deuteronomy, 190). In the light of this, is it not delightfully in character for Jesus to reveal himself alive first of all to despised women? And is it not totally incredible that if anybody had been fabricating the account of the resurrection they would have made its first witnesses women, people unqualified to give evidence?

The inclusion of Paul in the list is curious. The appearances ceased with the ascension of Jesus before the coming of the Spirit at Pentecost. It is as if Jesus spent six weeks showing them that he was indeed risen from the dead, training them for the world mission that awaited them, and then made a decisive break. From now on he would be known by the presence of his Spirit in their hearts, not by appearances to a limited number of people at occasional times. But Paul was persuaded that the Lord made an exception in his own case.

Doubt it if you will. He did not doubt it. And he knew a vision when he saw one. As a matter of fact he regularly had visions, as he shows in 2 Corinthians 12:1ff., and he was clear that this was no vision. It left him physically blinded for a few days. Jesus was seen by him alone, but those with him heard the voice (Acts 9:7). He knew this appearance to him was an exception. The Lord appeared 'last of all to me, as to one untimely born' (1 Corinthians 15:8), to commission this one-time opponent for the world mission which would make him Christ's most dedicated apostle. It is perhaps a reminder that however tidy your system, you can't get God taped.

Very well, there were these appearances. But what if they were hallucinations, seeming real enough to the people concerned, but devoid of objective reality?

The hallucination theory is at first sight attractive, but it is quite inadequate to explain the rise of the Christian movement, and it has serious weaknesses.

In the first place, only certain types of people are normally subject to hallucinations. Someone like Mary Magdalene might fill the bill, but scarcely men with as diverse temperaments as Peter, Thomas, James and Paul!

Hallucinations are normally individual things. A man may believe he is a poached egg, but it is rare to find that many people from many different backgrounds all suffer from the same delusion. Here the same 'hallucination' is observed by fishermen, tax-collectors, rabbis, close relations and five hundred people at once.

Hallucinations generally come to people who have been hankering after something for ages. The wish becomes father to the thought. But here we find no wish-fulfilment. As we have seen, the disciples were not expecting anything of the sort, and they were most reluctant to accept even the evidence of their own eyes.

Hallucinations tend to recur over a long period. Someone who suffers from obsessions continues to suffer from them. But here they ceased as dramatically as they began. It all took place within six weeks.

Hallucinations are generally restricted to a particular person, a particular time and a particular place. In this case, the diversity could scarcely have been wider. The appearance took place at early morning, at noon, at night. Seashore, roadside, upper room, garden – the locality made no difference. And those who experienced these 'seeings' were a very varied bunch.

The appearances did not become increasingly bizarre, as is often the case with hallucinations. Rather, they remained very restrained in character. Almost matter of fact. Moreover, far from mounting in frequency and pitch, as hallucinations often do, these meetings ceased entirely after forty days, never to recur.

The appearances seem to have an order and a logic about them. They start in the garden by the tomb itself; they progress in Jerusalem and its environs; they move into Galilee on mountain and lake, and they direct the disciples to a mission into the whole world after their Lord is taken from them. These meetings, in fact, make plain Jesus' determination to leave them, assure them of his presence with them wherever they go, and prepare them for the worldwide commission. When these functions of the resurrection appearances had been achieved, the need for them ceased. From now on the Jesus who had walked the streets of Palestine, the Jesus who had died and risen again, was with them by his Spirit in their hearts. That was the meaning of Pentecost. And Pentecost was the birthday of world mission.

3. THE CHRISTIAN CHURCH

All over the world there exists a body called the church. It numbers somewhere in the region of 1,800 million people.

I am certainly not going to argue 'so many can't be wrong'. Numbers do not demonstrate truth.

But it is not without significance that Christianity traces its own origin to the resurrection of Jesus Christ. The church came into being around AD 30 because the first Christians were convinced that Jesus Christ was alive again. Had it not been for that, they would have scattered to their homes and forgotten all about their three years with Jesus. They would certainly not have founded a movement which withstood all the syncretism of ancient religion, triumphed over scepticism and persecution, and became the one element in Roman civilization to survive the fall of Rome and spread into all the world.

It could be that these Christians had got something! It could be that they were right in their radiant conviction that Jesus was alive from the dead, and that in his resurrection they had found the key to understanding the universe.

The rise of the church is undeniable. It is possible, of course, to maintain that they were wrong to trace their origins to the resurrection of Jesus, but that denial leaves us with some awkward questions to answer.

What else can account for the beginnings of the church?
Let us suppose for a moment that Jesus did not rise, and that the disciples eventually recovered from the shock of his death enough to form a 'Society of Jesus Veterans'. They would have cherished old memories, and talked (and written) of all he had done during those brief three years when they had known him. They would have said little publicly: that would have been to invite mockery. Their 'guru' had, after all, ended up in failure and disgrace on a gibbet. And what would they have had to proclaim, anyhow? As for suggesting that others should cast in their lot with Jesus, that would have been unthinkable: he was dead and gone.

But, as we know, what happened was the very reverse of this. They did not gather to remember a dead Jesus but to celebrate a living one. In their letters they did not write about what he did in days gone by: but of what he, as Lord of the universe, was doing now. They did not even write their memoirs (or Gospels) until nearly a generation later when they were beginning to die off. Why not? They were too busy going round the world introducing people to the living Christ!

The growth and origin of the church is totally incredible if the resurrection is not true. Faith in the resurrection was the thing that differentiated them from the

Jewish establishment. But it was something they would not – they could not – give up. It happened to be true. It was the springboard for all their action.

What else can account for their success?
The whole theme of their preaching was the resurrection, and it was proclaimed initially within a few minutes' walk of the tomb where Jesus had lain.

How can we explain the many thousands who became believers, despite all that officialdom could do to stop them? How do we account for the fact that 'a large company of the priests became obedient to the faith' (Acts 6:7)? How do we account for the fact that Saul, the great persecutor of the church, was converted and became the greatest champion of the resurrection faith which he had laboured so hard to destroy? How do we explain the fact that, unlike any other event in the past which loses its dynamism the further distance you are from it, this has not happened with the resurrection? More people would die for this belief today than at any other time in history. Indeed, more *have* died.

I find it inconceivable that the church should have spread so fast and so widely had it been the case that the basic premise on which it was all founded, the resurrection, was false.

What else can explain their sacraments?
As all the world knows, Christians have two ceremonies which are integral to their life and faith. One is baptism, the sacrament of Christian initiation. The other is the Holy Communion, the sacrament of Christian growth. Both are rooted fairly and squarely in the resurrection.

Baptism was seen by the early Christians as re-enacting and personally appropriating the death and resurrection of Jesus: as the candidate goes into the water he dies to the old self-centred life and rises to a new life with Christ. 'All of us who have been baptized into Christ Jesus were baptized into his death. We were buried therefore with him by baptism into death, so that as Christ was raised from the dead by the glory of the Father, we too might walk in newness of life' (Romans 6:3ff.).

How could they have faced going through with a travesty like that if Jesus had in fact not risen from the dead?

It was the same with 'the Lord's Supper', as they called it. It was the Lord's not simply because it was held in memory of his sacrificial death on the cross, but because the Lord was present in their midst as they celebrated it. That is why we read that they broke bread with *agalliasis*, exultation (Acts 2:46). Unlike all the Greek community-feasts in honour of a dead hero, they rejoiced to share in communion with a living Lord. You could not take part in the Lord's Supper without having the truth made crystal clear to you in the very action of the service.

What else can explain the change from Saturday to Sunday? Go to Israel today if you want to see how Jews guard their day of rest. It is a lesson to us all. They will not allow transport or any work on *shabbat*, the sabbath. It is sacred to the Lord. It is the day to commemorate his rest after creation. But these Christians (all of them Jews, by the way) managed to change the very day of rest from Saturday to Sunday. Why? Because Sunday was the day when Jesus rose from the dead, and they reckoned that it was even more important to honour the day death died than the day life began.

It would be hard, very hard, to change the day off from Sunday to Monday these days . . . yet we in the West have no such emotional and theological attachment to our day off as the Jews had, and have. Imagine how incredibly difficult it must have been to make such a change from the heart of Judaism. Yet that is what

happened. It must have required some simply staggering happening to trigger such a thing off.

The New Testament gives us one – the resurrection.

*What else can explain the Christian conviction that Jesus is
Lord?*

The earliest Christians, Jews to a man, were the most
ardent of monotheists. Yet they acclaimed Jesus as
divine. He was called 'Lord', 'My Lord and my God',
'the Lamb who was slain and is in the midst of the
throne', 'the Son of God' and other such titles. He was
put on a par with God Almighty – and that *by Jews* of
all people! This simply blows the mind.

How could they have been driven to the conviction
that God Almighty had visited them in and through
the person of Jesus? The answer must lie in the resurrection. He was 'descended from David according to
the flesh', so ran an ancient Christian creed, quoted by
Paul in Romans 1:3ff., 'and designated Son of God in
power . . . by his resurrection from the dead'.

That was it. That is why they served him as his
'slaves', for so they delighted to call themselves. That
is why they did not shrink from offering him worship.

Another ancient creed, springing from the days of
the Aramaic-speaking church, puts it like this:

*Christ Jesus, though he was in the form of God, did not
count equality with God a thing to be grasped, but emptied
himself, taking the form of a servant, being born in the
likeness of men. And being found in human form he hum-
bled himself and became obedient unto death, even death on
a cross. Therefore God has highly exalted him and bestowed
on him the name which is above every name, that at the
name of Jesus every knee should bow, in heaven and on
earth and under the earth, and every tongue confess that
Jesus Christ is Lord, to the glory of God the Father.*

Philippians 2:6–11

And just to rub it in, we must remember that every new Christian had to confess 'Jesus is Lord' in his baptism. It is the earliest baptismal confession of the Christian church. And it is totally incomprehensible without the resurrection.

The resurrection, of course, cannot be proved. No historical event can. All one can do is to show that there is such a convergence of historical probabilities that the truth of the resurrection is placed beyond all reasonable doubt. In his book *The Resurrection of Christ*, A. M. Ramsey, later to become Archbishop of Canterbury, shows that 'certain historical facts are unaccountable apart from the resurrection, and that different lines of historical testimony so converge as to point to the resurrection with overwhelming probability'. It is, as Leslie Weatherhead once put it in *The Resurrection and the Life*, as if 'half a dozen signposts, with the name of the same village painted on them, all point one way. Then sincerity in regard to the evidence compels belief that the village exists, even though we have never been there.'

But the strongest evidence for the resurrection remains for the next chapter. It is afforded by those who *have* 'been there'.

4

Meeting the Master

If the title of this chapter sounds a bit pious, you must forgive me. The fact of the matter is that personal encounter with Jesus Christ is the most powerful indicator that he rose from the dead.

Consider the earliest disciples. They took to the streets on the Day of Pentecost, seven weeks after the events of Holy Week. That delay alone would be very surprising had they been perpetrating a fraud. They were becoming acquainted with the risen Christ and then, obedient to his command, awaited the coming of his Spirit into their lives.

At Pentecost he came. And the disciples thereupon caused a major disturbance in the temple courts. People thought they were drunk. But Peter, their spokesman, replied in effect, 'That is nonsense. It is too early in the day to be drunk! But what God promised long ago has come true. He has given us his Spirit, the Spirit that lives in Jesus, whom you wickedly killed, but whom God has wonderfully raised from the dead. This is what accounts for the change you have noticed in us.'

That was the thrust of Peter's speech that day. He and his friends were, as he aptly describes it, 'witnesses to the resurrection'. Three thousand Jews were convinced by what he said, and they became Christians that very day.

These disciples had come alive in a big way. Gone

re the crippling inhibitions that had kept them quiet in the previous seven weeks: they now preached ceaselessly. Gone was the cowardice which had kept them hidden away in the upper room: they were now as bold as brass for what they knew to be true. Neither prison, persecution, nor the threat of death could silence them. Many of them sealed their testimony with their blood.

Knowing the risen Christ to be in their midst, they even overcame their instinct for private ownership, and shared their possessions with one another in a practical and loving communalism.

These were changed men, and all Jerusalem knew it.

It was just the same when the gospel spread to pagan soil. In Athens the testimony of Christians caused a public debate (Acts 17). There was something new about them: the Athenians themselves put it down to 'Jesus and the resurrection'. At Philippi (Acts 16) their impact was so great that a riot ensued and they were put into prison. Result? They sang hymns at midnight, and the gaoler and his family were converted! They made a big dent in the pagan licentiousness of Corinth, a city which was a byword for immorality. Many of the people who became Christians there had been involved in every kind of vice. But the power of the Spirit changed them. 'Neither the immoral, nor idolaters, nor adulterers, nor sexual perverts, nor thieves, nor the greedy, nor drunkards, nor revilers, nor robbers will inherit the kingdom of God' wrote Paul. '*And such were some of you*. But you were washed, you were sanctified, you were justified in the name of the Lord Jesus Christ and in the Spirit of our God' (1 Corinthians 6:9ff.).

Such was the power of the living Christ. He could transform shameless pleasure-seekers, criminals, abandoned, self-centred people, and turn them into the church at Corinth. If the gospel could do that for the rakes at Corinth, then it spoke volumes for the truth of the resurrection.

It was to these same Corinthians that Paul wrote that fascinating piece about the resurrection which we have already examined (1 Cor. 15, see page 10). But we left one thing out. We did not look at the change of life which that short chronicle reveals. Paul tells them that 'Christ died for our sins in accordance with the scriptures, that he was buried, that he was raised on the third day in accordance with the scriptures, and that he appeared to Cephas, then to the twelve. Then he appeared to more than five hundred brethren at one time, most of whom are still alive, though some have fallen asleep. Then he appeared to James, then to all the apostles. Last of all . . . he appeared also to me.'

What are these early witnesses saying? Not that they saw Jesus rise: it is one of the marks of the truthfulness of the New Testament that *nobody* claims that – whereas any fabricator could hardly have resisted producing eyewitnesses for such a *dénouement*. No, they make a more sober but in the end more far-reaching claim.

They bear witness to the fact that Jesus not only rose but *is alive*.

That comes out clearly in the tenses used in this remarkable ancient document. 'Died', 'was buried' and 'appeared' are all in the aorist tense, the normal tense for past action. But the verb translated 'he was raised to life' stands out like a sore thumb, for it is in the perfect tense. And the perfect is used when a past action has effects which remain until the present. So in that single word *egēgertai* we see two crucial points. Not only did he rise again from the dead on the third day, as a fact of history; *he is still alive*, and can be encountered. Such was the earliest Christian conviction about the resurrection, embedded in this document which derives from the thirties of the first century.

That is an absolutely staggering claim. What witnesses does Paul adduce to support it?

First 'he appeared to Cephas (Peter)'. That interview

the risen Jesus changed Peter from a vacillating, bastic failure into the courageous leader whom we et in the Acts, the man on whose testimony and example the early church was built.

Then 'the twelve' come before us to give their testimony. They turned from a rabble, who deserted their leader at his hour of trial, into the church that was not afraid to face lions in the arena, or execution from the government of their nation. For them, death was a defeated foe.

Thirdly, we are presented with James. He was the brother of Jesus (Mark 6:3), the child of Joseph and Mary, or maybe of Joseph by a former marriage. He was not a believer in Jesus during the days of his public ministry. Far from it. Jesus' brothers did not believe in him: the whole family thought him deranged (John 7:5; Mark 3:21). But James too met with the risen Jesus. And he was dramatically changed by that encounter. He became the leader of the Jerusalem church.

Paul mentions that he appeared to 'all the apostles'. This would include Thomas, who was not with the disciples when Jesus first met them after his resurrection. But he was with them the second time. And he was invited to stretch out his finger and put it into the hole in Jesus' hands, and to stretch out his hand and thrust it into the spear-wound in his side. I don't suppose he needed to. He fell at the feet of Jesus, we are told, transformed by that resurrection encounter from sceptic to passionate follower. 'My Lord and my God', he cried. He was a different man from that day onwards. There is a strong tradition that he took the gospel to the south of India, where the ancient Mar Thoma Church exists to this day.

The 'five hundred brethren at one time' are interesting. Some of them had died by the time Paul wrote to the Corinthians in AD 53. But most of them were still alive, he says. They must have been Galilean followers of Jesus who had known him during his ministry, and had no doubt witnessed many of the events recorded in the Gospels. We hear no more about them. They are the forerunners of the hordes of nameless Christians who have been bearing witness to the risen Christ ever since. To such he is no dead historical figure, but a living contemporary, the supreme reality of their lives, with whom they share every experience and converse every day.

This is what Paul found Jesus to be. After years of service for the risen Master he could say artlessly, 'I *know* whom I have believed' (2 Timothy 1:12). He did not simply know about Jesus. He knew him. That original encounter changed his life and launched him into a relationship as intimate and daily renewed as marriage. His goal in life was simply this: to know Jesus better (Philippians 3:10).

Any real Christian can say the same.

I can.

I well recall the day in my teens when I passed from *knowing about* Jesus to *knowing* him. I believed in a vague sort of way that he had risen, but it meant nothing to me. And then I was brought face to face with a number of teachers and fellow pupils in my school to whom it clearly meant a lot. I watched them. I observed the differences that this relation with Christ made in their lives. I wanted what they had got. And one day I tentatively asked how I could find it. I came to see that if Jesus rose from the dead then he was alive, and I could meet him. Hesitantly, I put my life in his hands, as best I knew how. And I have proved the reality of his presence ever since. It has gradually become the greatest certainty of my life.

Perhaps you think, 'It's all very well for you. You are a minister.' True enough, but I should never have dreamed of becoming one had I not found that Jesus is alive.

However, I shall be glad to give you some twentieth-century witnesses who are not ministers.

Michelle is a white South African graduate, a highly
intelligent mathematician. She was born into a Jewish
family, but in the course of her studies at Cape Town
University had been impressed by the Christians she
knew. She came to encounter the living Christ for her-
self, and that meeting changed her life. She wrote at
the time of her baptism, 'I think this is one of the most
wonderful facets of Christianity, the great joy it brings.
When I was telling someone else about it over the
phone, they said they could *hear* how happy I
sounded . . . Before my baptism I was scared to admit
to my Jewish friends that I was a Christian, but now I
want the whole world to know.' And now guess where
she is? Married to a Christian and working with him as
a missionary in Kenya. Quite a change for a white South
African!

I think of a group of unemployed boys in Lima, Peru.
Unemployed, that is, until the Christians began to set
up a small leather-work shop for them to learn a trade
in. They got a new leather-work teacher. And their first
enquiry? 'Is he a brother?' He was not, in the sense
they meant it. So they set about introducing him to
the living Christ. Even in their deprived background,
friendship with Jesus was the paramount concern of
their lives.

I think of an Ethiopian, who came up to Oxford to
study, and came to faith in the risen Christ. He was
thrilled with the Lord, and enthusiastic in speaking
about him to his fellow overseas students.

A Polish girl who lives in Warsaw comes from a mili-
tantly atheistic home. She was invited to a meeting of
Christian young people and was fascinated by their
evident joy as they spoke of Jesus. Soon afterwards she
happened to sit next to a Christian on a bus. He spoke
simply to her about the risen Christ and secretly she

believed. She found in her own heart the reality of which the others had spoken, and after a week she plucked up courage to tell her parents. They were furious. She was kicked out of house and home. But it did not rob her of her peace of mind, and her infectious joy. The result? Her parents are now asking questions. They want what she has got.

This is how a university teacher in computing science has described to me her appreciation of the encounter with Christ that has changed her life:

The best thing that has ever happened to me was the dawning awareness that Jesus Christ was not just a historic figure; a good man dead and gone. Mysterious though it seems, he is the Son of God, who died on behalf of all, rose from the dead, and now offers life to any who dares to trust him. I have taken this step of faith. I know I am alive. Jesus has brought strong and consistent meaning to my life. More than anything in the world I want to live my life for him. I want him to be my Number One. Walking with Jesus through life is the most liberating of all possible relationships. Jesus understands me better than I can ever hope to understand myself. Gradually he is releasing me from my 'hang-ups' and enabling me to discover and to become the person he wants me to be. His capacity for loving and forgiving is endless. He forgives me even when I cannot forgive myself. Nothing can ever separate him from me, so I am never alone.

If Jesus were not alive I could not be writing as I am. His love for me brings a security and hope in this unstable and changing world. Living for him, motivated and helped by his Spirit within, is the biggest challenge anyone could be given. Perhaps the words of Dame Julian best express what I feel most deeply:

If everything is lost, thanks be to God.
If I must see it go, watch it go,
Watch it fade away, die,
Thanks be to God that he is all I have
And if I have him not, I have nothing at all.

This is the sort of testimony that many of our contemporaries bear to Jesus Christ. They speak of what they actually know from their own experience of Jesus.

That may not seem very satisfactory. It might be tidier if it were possible to prove the matter one way or the other. But life is not like that. It simply is not possible to put into words an experience which has changed your life, let alone to prove it. That is what a Ghanaian friend of mine was struggling to say when he wrote: 'I know Jesus lives, because I meet him every day, and share fellowship with him. Fellowship can only exist between people who are *living*. I think that the truth that Jesus lives is something that one can experience rather than describe.'

That is true enough. And it is borne out by this story a Czechoslovak theologian told me. A Russian lecturer, a member of the Communist party, was addressing a packed audience on the subject of the resurrection of Jesus Christ. He spoke at considerable length, seeking to discredit it. At the end, an Orthodox priest rose and asked if he might reply. He was warned that he could have only five minutes. 'Five seconds is all I shall need' was his reply. He turned to the audience, and gave the delightful Easter greeting, characteristic of the Eastern church. '*Christos anestē*', he cried, 'Christ is risen.' Back with a deafening roar came the traditional reply from the crowded hall, '*Alethōs anestē*', 'Truly he is risen.'

That is the essence of the Christian witness down the centuries. It has not changed since some of the disciples encountered Jesus on the first Easter day.

The heart of the matter for the Christian is this: Jesus

did not merely rise, he is alive. Alive and ready to be met by men, women or children who are willing to share their lives with him.

That is not the common image of Christianity. God forgive us, we have smothered the risen Christ in denominationalism, ecclesiasticism, respectability, moralism and goodness knows what else. But that is the heart of authentic Christianity.

Christians are the 'community of the resurrection'. They are like iron filings attracted to and adhering to the magnetic person of Jesus Christ, risen from the dead.

It is impossible to do justice to the evidence for the resurrection unless you take into account this world-wide testimony from believers great and small that Jesus is not a dead hero, but a living Lord. The changes he can make to life at all levels will be the subject of our next chapter.

5

Drawing the Implications

The resurrection of Jesus was never intended to be a matter for academic discussion. It has the most practical of implications, and ought never to be considered apart from them.

When Paul discusses the resurrection in 1 Corinthians 15 he shows a ruthless integrity in drawing the implications. If Jesus did not rise from the grave, then Paul's preaching has been a waste of time, their faith is futile, and they remain unforgiven. What is more, all Christians misrepresent God, dead Christians are finished and live Christians are deluded! That is how he summarizes the situation in verses 12–19 of that chapter.

On the other hand, if Christ did rise, he is alive to be encountered (verses 4ff.), he has cleared our accusing past (verse 3), he has broken the fear of death (verse 54), his resurrection is the pledge of our own (verse 22), he can change human nature (verse 57), and he has a plan for our lives (verse 58). In other words, it is impossible to exaggerate the importance, for practical everyday concerns, of the resurrection of Jesus from the dead.

Let us take a look at some of the implications of the resurrection.

The resurrection shows that death is not the end

For centuries men and women have been wrestling with the question: is death the end? Are we snuffed out like a candle, or is death the doorway to some future life? There are plenty of arguments, plenty of speculations, plenty of *séances*. But there would be only one certain way to find out. That is if someone had died and had come back – not just to die again in due course, but as the undisputed conqueror of death.

Jesus Christ has achieved just that. He has returned from the grave and has demonstrated that there is indeed a life after death. If we insist on reckoning without that factor of life after death, we are being foolishly shortsighted. For by his resurrection Jesus has 'forced open a door that had been locked since the death of the first man. He has met, fought, and beaten the king of death. Everything is different because he has done so. This is the beginning of the new creation: a new chapter in cosmic history has opened.' So wrote C. S. Lewis in *Miracles*.

It is the sober truth, ever since the day death died. For, enigmatic though it seems, that is precisely what happened. Death has had its fangs drawn, its finality reversed.

No longer need men face death as Dylan Thomas advised:

Do not go gentle into that good night,
Old age should burn and rave at close of day;
Rage, rage against the dying of the light.

In days gone by there was nothing to look for but

. . . the dread of something after death,
The undiscovered country from whose bourne
No traveller returns.

But now a traveller has returned. It is no longer an

undiscovered country. Easter spelt the day when death, in all its fearsome finality, died, and a way was opened up to that country of eternal life for which so many had longed, but of whose existence there was no clear proof.

The resurrection shows which religion to follow

Ours is a day of syncretism. All religions are commonly thought to be much the same. It is not supposed to matter which you choose. But Christianity refuses to be sucked into this indifferentism. It always has done.

Is this because Christians are uncharitable and narrowminded? Not at all. It is simply that Jesus Christ claimed to be the way to God, the truth about God and the very life of God. He vindicated that claim by the resurrection. Jesus said 'All things have been delivered to me by my Father; and no-one knows the Son except the Father, and no-one knows the Father except the Son and any one to whom the Son chooses to reveal him' (Matthew 11:27). A staggering claim, but one which he made good by the resurrection.

The resurrection, therefore, is the place to begin if you are looking for a satisfying faith on which to base your life. Do not waste a lot of time investigating every religion under the sun from animism to Hinduism. Examine the evidence for the resurrection of Jesus Christ instead. If he is risen you need look no further.

You will, of course, find much to admire, much to learn from, in other religions (as well as a lot of filth and cruelty): the God of the whole earth has not left himself without witness. But you will not find in them anything good and true which cannot be found in Christ. And nowhere else will you find out about a God who cares enough for you to die for you, to rise from the grave as a pledge of your future, and to be willing to come and share his life with you.

If Jesus is, as the resurrection asserts, God himself come to our rescue, then to reject him, or even to ignore him, is ultimate folly. That is why Jesus is not, and never can be, just one among the many religious leaders of mankind. He is not even the best. He is the only. Among many examples of the relative he stands out as the absolute. In the risen Jesus, God Almighty confronts us with shattering directness. He offers us total succour; but he asks of us total allegiance.

It is sensible to have an interest in comparative religion, but the more you know of the others, the more clearly Christianity is seen to be unique. And the heart of Christianity is the resurrection.

The point is well made by the famous meeting of Auguste Comte, the French philosopher, and Thomas Carlyle. Comte said he intended to found a new religion, which would sweep away Christianity and everything else in its wake. He was very enthusiastic about it. Carlyle's devastating reply ran something like this: 'Splendid. All you need to do is to speak as never man spoke, to live as never man lived, to be crucified, rise again the third day, and get the world to believe you are still alive. Then your religion will have some chance of success.'

The resurrection shows Jesus is the Son of God

Jesus made many remarkable claims during his lifetime. He claimed the right to forgive sins (Mark 2:10) and to accept worship (Luke 5:8); he claimed he would separate sheep and goats at the last judgment (Matthew 25:31ff.); he claimed to be the light of the world, the bread of life and the resurrection (John 8:12; 6:48; 11:25).

Many people did not believe him. So he made his credibility hang on the resurrection. Refusing their request for a compulsive sign, Jesus said, 'An evil and adulterous generation seeks for a sign; but no sign shall be given to it except the sign of the prophet Jonah. For as Jonah was three days and three nights in the belly of the whale, so will the Son of man be three days and three nights in the heart of the earth' (Matthew 12:38ff.).

And from the earliest days after the resurrection, his followers began to realize the staggering implications. He fulfilled all the hopes of the Old Testament scriptures! So he *was* the prophet like Moses, he *was* the Son of man of whom Daniel had prophesied, he *was* the Suffering Servant of Isaiah, he *was* the Messiah, so long awaited by the Jews. All this and more. He was no less than God's 'Son' – distinct from the heavenly Father and yet one with him. Peter proclaimed this as early as the Day of Pentecost. Paul cited the early creed we have already looked at, in Romans 1:3–4: he was 'descended from David according to the flesh and designated Son of God in power . . . by his resurrection'. In his own words Paul maintains 'In him dwells all the fullness of the godhead in bodily form' (Colossians 2:9).

So Jesus was not just a great teacher and a splendid man. He was no latter-day Confucius, no Jewish edition of Socrates. He was shown by the resurrection to be no less than he claimed to be, the Saviour, the Messiah, the Son of man, the Son of God, the way to God. Because Christ rose to a new and eternal life, he can no longer be classified among men of excellence. He was indeed completely human: but he is nothing less than God. And as God he claims our worship and our allegiance.

The resurrection shows that the cross atoned for our sins
The New Testament is insistent that 'all have sinned and fall short of the glory of God', that 'none is righteous, no, not one', and that 'all the world is guilty before God' (Romans 3:23, 10, 19). That is unpalatable, but we know it is true.

We also know that even if we could live a perfect life from now on, that could do nothing to wipe out the past. Reluctantly we assent to the humbling verdict of the Bible: 'No man can deliver his own soul' (Psalm 49:7).

But, as Jesus told us, he came 'to give his life as a

ransom for many' (Matthew 20:28). And on the cross he did just that. The darkness at Calvary gives us an insight into the darkness that stifled his soul when 'the Lord laid on him the iniquity of us all', as the prophet Isaiah had predicted centuries before.

Peter, who was perhaps an eyewitness at the edge of the crowd, picked up that theme of Isaiah's and declared, 'He himself bore our sins in his own body on the tree' and again 'Christ also died for sins once for all, the righteous for the unrighteous, that he might bring us to God' (1 Peter 2:24; 3:18).

All the New Testament writers agree. This is what the cross means: God has not abandoned us – rather, he has himself undertaken the enormous ransom, the vast debt incurred by human sinfulness. Well might John write 'God is love . . . not that we loved God but that he loved us and sent his Son to be the expiation for our sins' (1 John 4:8, 10).

But was his sacrifice enough? Was even the death of the Son of God sufficient cover, so to speak, for all our liabilities? Could God Almighty, as the hymn puts it, justly 'look on him and pardon me'?

There would have been no way of answering that question had not Jesus risen from the dead. We could not have been sure whether his death-cry, 'It is finished' (John 19:30), was a cry of defeat or a shout of victory. But the resurrection made it crystal clear. The resurrection was God's 'Yes' to the achievement of Calvary. It was God's vindication of his precious Son. It was the demonstration that he could, because of what Jesus did on Calvary, forgive (indeed, acquit) any who came to him trusting in what Jesus had done. He was 'put to death for our trespasses and raised for our justification'. Such is the triumphal conclusion of Romans 4:25.

All down the ages the cross and resurrection have spelt peace for troubled consciences. I shall never forget the joy on the face of one student when he understood it. He had in fact made a list of the things burdening his conscience, and had brought it along with him. But as he came to understand what Jesus through his cross and resurrection had done to his failures, there was only one thing to do with that list: we tore it into little pieces!

John Bunyan expressed it picturesquely in *Pilgrim's Progress:*

> As Christian came up with the cross, his burden loosed from off his shoulders and fell from his back. It began to tumble, and continued to do so till it came to the mouth of the sepulchre where it fell in, and I saw it no more.
>
> Then was Christian glad and lightsome, and said with a merry heart, 'He hath given me rest by his sorrow, and life by his death'. . . . Then Christian gave three leaps for joy, and went on singing.

That is how it appeared to John Bunyan three hundred years ago in Bedford prison. This is how it appears to Michael Alison, a British politician:

> My conviction about the certainty of the resurrection is based upon the profound sense of forgiveness which I enjoy, in dissociating myself from the dark deeds I have done or might do, and associating them with the dead and mutilated Christ. My 'old self' is, in a way I can actually experience with inward conviction, done away with, and destroyed in Christ. The profoundest element in my fellowship with God lies precisely in this: that he can allow himself to be destroyed by the worst in me, and yet can come back loving! Without the actual fellowship of loving God in Christ, the past transference of guilt would be a mere expediency, a cause for deepening, not relieving, self-centredness and remorse.

The resurrection offers us continual companionship

The final promise of Jesus Christ, recorded in the last verse of Matthew's Gospel, is this: 'Lo, I am with you always, to the close of the age.'

His followers are promised no sinecure, no safe passage. But they are told that whatever befalls them cannot rob them of his presence.

Paul was acutely aware of this. As he lay in prison he was able to write 'Rejoice in the Lord always; again I will say, Rejoice. . . . The Lord is at hand' (Philippians 4:4ff.). And when he was reflecting on the enormous forces of opposition which he and his mission for Christ had stirred up, he took comfort from this fact, that the living Lord was with him, and would be to the end. 'Who shall separate us from the love of Christ? Shall tribulation, or distress, or persecution, or famine, or nakedness, or peril, or sword?' (Romans 8:35). Christ offers us his constant presence, and no other security.

But that offer is enough. For loneliness is a killer. You can be more lonely in a crowd than on a desert island. Loneliness is one of the main causes of suicide among students, of despair among the old. It is not surprising that the famous painter Annigoni, when asked what picture he would most like to be remembered by, replied 'Solitude'. He was so impressed by the loneliness of modern man that he has painted no less than twelve studies of it.

Jesus promised to meet this gnawing need by his presence in the hearts and lives of his followers: he even offered to become our friend. 'I have called you friends' he says (John 15:15), and that friendship is beyond value. Charles Kingsley was once asked the most significant thing in his experience, and he replied enigmatically 'I had a Friend'.

Somebody expressed it to me a little more explicitly thus: 'Jesus is the only person with whom I can communicate in every situation, knowing immediately that he has understood completely. . . . I find it difficult to believe that he loves me and cares about the smallest as well as the largest details of my life; that he is willing and able to forgive me time after time for doing what I know to be wrong. But experience has shown that all this is true, and I am assured it always will be.'

That friendship with Christ is what enables the Christian to be somewhat independent of the approval or disapproval of the crowd. He is not squeezed into the conventional mould by the pressures of public opinion or social custom. He has a friend, and in that friendship lies his security. So 'keep your life free from love of money, and be content with what you have; for he has said "I will never fail you nor forsake you." Hence we can confidently say, "The Lord is my helper, I will not be afraid; what can man do to me?" ' (Hebrews 13:5ff.).

The resurrection affords moral power
Our trouble is not only our guilt and loneliness, but our inability to do what is right. Like the apostle Paul we have so often to admit 'I can will what is right, but I cannot do it. For I do not do the good I want, but the evil I do not want is what I do' (Romans 7:18ff.). There is a moral weakness in every one of us, and try as we may, we cannot eradicate it.

But this is where the power of the risen Christ comes in. He lived a perfect life, and if he comes to share life with us, we can surely turn to him in moments of temptation and ask for his strength to take over and replace our weakness. 'I can do anything', wrote Paul, 'through him who gives me strength' (Philippians 4:13).

There is a most illuminating prayer of his, recorded in his letter to Christians at Ephesus (1:19ff.). He prays that they may know 'what is the immeasurable greatness of his power in us who believe, according to the working of his great might which he accomplished in Christ when he raised him from the dead'. In other words, the very power which was exerted by God in raising Christ from the dead is available to raise us from the failures to which we are so prone by nature.

History is full of examples which show the truth of this wonderful promise. Men like Augustine and John Newton, deeply sunk in vice, became models of Christian living once they surrendered to the power of the living Christ.

In my own experience as a Christian, I have seen him transform the lives of prostitutes, drug addicts, swindlers, and people caught in the toils of the occult. I have seen compulsive gamblers and alcoholics changed. His touch has still its ancient power.

There is nothing automatic about it. He does not give us power if we do not want it and ask for it: and often we don't. Moreover, we do not become Christlike all at once. This is a gradual process of transformation.

Nevertheless, the power of the living Jesus is well able to handle any specific temptation which we hand over to him, and to give us power to overcome it. In this way we become 'more than conquerors through him who loved us' (Romans 8:37). Conquerors – yes. But *more than* conquerors, because through the conflict and the temptation we learn to trust him more and get to know him better. So let none of us think our temptations are too great to bear. They are not too great for him to bear. 'No temptation has overtaken you that is not common to man. God is faithful, and he will not let you be tempted beyond your strength, but with the temptation will also provide the way of escape, that you may be able to endure it' (1 Corinthians 10:13). The 'way of escape' is to ask him for his strength, early on in the process of temptation, *and really to want it!*

The resurrection brings joy
It brought joy to the first disciples when Jesus rose and made himself known to them. It still does. He told them that joy would be his parting gift to them, and so it has proved. The pages of Christian history re-echo with joy

and laughter, for he does not come alongside us in order to rob us or make us miserable, but to give us life at its very best. 'I came that they may have life, and have it abundantly' he said (John 10:10). And that is in striking contrast to the disenchantment and dissatisfaction which are such notable features of our day.

There is normally a tremendous sense of joy when a person turns his life over to Jesus Christ. Of course: the long resistance is over, and the creature is reconciled with his Creator. But that initial excitement does not last, any more than it does in marriage. It gives way to something less bubbly and more profound: a deep sense of contentment.

A bedridden man suffering from an incurable disease wrote of this inner contentment: 'Christ has made it possible for me to accept suffering without inner resentment, bitternness or boredom. Those are the burdens he has taken from me. He has given me in return peace of heart, joy and illumination during the lonely hours, and a focus of attention always away from myself, because there is so much work to be done for him even when I am flat on my back.'

I have noticed this joy most, I think, among Christians who have few of the things we normally prize – money, security, a nice home. I have noticed it among the poor in the third world countries. I have noticed it among Christians in the face of death.

I think of a dear friend, Archbishop Janani Luwum of Uganda, who was martyred by President Amin. Janani had to tell Amin that the church could not go along with his murders and injustice: the President was furious and determined to make away with Janani. But the Archbishop did not quail, and he did not quit. He knew what was coming to him, and when, like his Master, he was arraigned and falsely accused, he said nothing, only gently shook his head in denial of the charges. When taken downstairs to the torture chamber, he found another believer, and together they fell on their knees to pray to God for their persecutor. That is what I mean by joy. There was a calm sense that all is in the hands of a loving God, and that nothing can separate the believer from the companionship of a living Christ. That is a joy worth having.

The resurrection introduces us to a community with a purpose
There is something very fragmentary about Western society. We think and act individualistically. God never intended us to live that way, but rather as a community in dependence on himself. The resurrection makes that possible.

It is noteworthy that in the Gospels the disciples were rescued from their loneliness and despair by the resurrection, and then each did not go off and do his own thing: we find them being together, praying and eating together, witnessing together on the street and in the synagogues. It is to the disciples *as a community* that Jesus gave his commission to go and spread the gospel throughout the world, according to both Matthew and John. It is to the disciples *as a community* that the Spirit came.

In a society that is falling apart, this aspect of the resurrection cannot be stressed too strongly. Once we get in touch with the living Christ he puts us deeply in touch with others in his church. Linked to the head, we inevitably take our place among other limbs in the body, and find the thrill of being caught up in Christ's mission.

I think of a small-time gardener in a Latin American country. Illiterate and ignorant, he could well be spending a very narrow life. But far from it. He is the lay pastor of a tiny church, some twenty strong, which meets in his house. All the members share what Christ is doing in their lives, and they are growing in love and usefulness. The risen Christ has not only come into this man's individual life: he has made him into what he was intended to be, and put him in touch both with his God and his fellow believers.

I think of a sophisticated university lecturer who, when first I knew him, was arrogant and critical. But now it is all very different. He has come to a deep trust in the living Christ, and the results in his own life have been remarkable. Gone is that old critical attitude. Gone is the proud isolation. He is very much part of the extraordinarily mixed local church community to which he belongs, and one of the parish house groups meets in his home. He sees himself as part of a community which is, for all its failings, a first instalment of God's kingdom, a community marked by the resurrection.

The resurrection of Christ is the pledge of our own
Jesus assured his disciples that he was going away at his death, to prepare for them a place in the Father's house. Had this not been the case, he would have told them (John 14:2ff.).

That was quite a claim. But it became credible after the resurrection of Jesus.

If he had risen to a new quality of life beyond the grave, there was good reason to suppose that he could bring his followers there too. Paul, therefore, can say 'Christ has been raised from the dead, the first fruits of those who have fallen asleep' (1 Corinthians 15:20). Where there are first fruits, there is also a crop to come. That is why the book of Revelation can exclaim 'Happy are the dead who die in the Lord' (Revelation 14:13). Death for the Christian is not, as society at large supposes, the worst thing that can befall you. It takes you out of one room in the Father's house, the room of faith, into another room, the room of sight. You will be with the Lord.

An old Christian man lay dying, and he asked his doctor, also a Christian, if he had any convictions about what lay before him after death. The doctor fumbled for an answer. Then there was heard a scratching at the door. 'Do you hear that?' he asked his patient. 'That is my dog. I left him downstairs, but he grew impatient and has come up here, and can hear my voice. He has no idea of what lies beyond this door, but he knows that I am here. Now is it not like that with you? You do not know what lies beyond the door, but you know your Master is there.'

What that life will be like we cannot say in any detail, nor need we try. Two hints are contained in 1 Corinthians 15. The first indicates that we shall be like Jesus. 'As we have borne the image of the man of dust, we shall also bear the image of the man of heaven' (15:49). The second indicates that the splendour of that life after death will be analogous to the whole ear of wheat compared to the shrivelled grain which was put into the ground (15:35–38). If you had never seen a plant of wheat growing, you would be amazed to discover that it came from that little dry grain which you had planted the previous autumn, would you not? Right, says Paul, it is like that with the resurrection. As with the wheat seed, there will be a continuity of life going right through the process of death. As with the wheat seed, the final state will be far more wonderful than the first. It will, in fact, be like the resurrection body of Jesus – identifiable, but no longer subject to the limitations of time and space and decay. And that is something to look forward to.

Christianity does not teach the immortality of the soul, but the resurrection of the body; not immediately we die, but at the last day. So there is no question of the flight of the alone to the Alone, or absorption into the archetypal One. It is rather a matter of personal and undying relationships between redeemed persons and their Lord. Nor is there a question of crass materialism, as if the very stuff of this present body were essential to our future state: 'God gives it a body as he has chosen. . . . There are heavenly bodies and there are earthly bodies; but the glory of the heavenly is one, and the glory of the earthly is another' (1 Corinthians 15:38–40).

There is a lovely passage where Martin Luther wrestles with the problem of life after death, and revels in the confidence that Christ's resurrection affords him:

> Just as one does not know how it happens that one falls asleep and suddenly morning approaches when one awakes, so we will suddenly be resurrected at the last day, not knowing how we have come into death and through death. We shall sleep until he comes and knocks at the tomb and says 'Dr. Martin, get up!' Then in one moment I will get up and will rejoice with him in eternity.

The resurrection can transform our attitude to death

Don't believe people if they tell you that they do not fear death. The fear of death grips modern civilization in a vice-like grip, and it is none the less real for being driven underground.

> Nor dread nor hope attend
> A dying animal;
> A man awaits his end
> Dreading and hoping all.
> W. B. Yeats, *Death*

But the wonderful thing about the resurrection of Jesus is that it gives a solid ground for hope. Here is one who has died and risen, and assures believers that they will be with him in the after-life. What is there to fear?

Paul put his finger on the really awesome thing about death: it finalizes our state of sinful rebellion against God, our constant breaking of his law. If he is just, then this is something he cannot overlook. But if Christ has borne our condemnation, then the fangs of death have been drawn. 'Death is swallowed up in victory.

O death, where is thy victory? O death, where is thy sting?' Paul is quoting the Old Testament. He then continues on his own account, 'The sting of death is sin, and the power of sin is the law. But thanks be to God, who gives us the victory through our Lord Jesus Christ' (1 Corinthians 15:54ff.).

The writer to the Hebrews eloquently makes the same point when he says that one of the main reasons why Jesus came to share our flesh and blood was 'that through death he might destroy him who has the power of death, that is, the devil, and deliver all those who through fear of death were subject to lifelong bondage' (Hebrews 2:14ff.).

The living Christ really does remove the fear of death.

I was very struck by the story of the first converts in Uganda a hundred years ago. Several were pages at the court of the Kabaka of Buganda, and they were arrested and burnt alive. They refused to deny Christ. Instead they burst into song – the hymn 'Daily, daily, sing the praises of the city God has made' – while the youngest, little Yusufu (only eleven years of age) said, 'Please do not cut off my arms. I will not struggle in the fire that takes me to Jesus.'

But it is not only our fear of death which the resurrection of Jesus can transform, but also our attitude to bereavement.

When a Christian loved one dies we need not be left desolate. We have three precious gifts. First, the promise of the risen Lord: 'Where I am there you shall be also.' That departed one is with the Lord, and is better off than we are. Secondly, we have the people of the risen Lord: he has given us brethren to 'rejoice with those that rejoice and weep with those that weep'. The Christian family can make an enormous and lasting difference to enduring and overcoming bereavement. And thirdly, we have the promise of the risen Lord: 'I am with you always.' We shall sorrow, to be sure, but not as those who have no hope. We shall weep, but not inconsolably. There will be a great reunion one day, and the pledge of that is the living Lord who holds both us and the dead believer in his grip, a grip which even death cannot break (see 1 Thessalonians 4:16–18).

I shall not soon forget a couple whose only daughter had been killed by a careless motorist shortly after she had come to Oxford to train as an occupational therapist. My friends were full of grief, but also full of hope – the living Lord was very real to them. We had a luncheon in my house for the funeral party after the service, and the father spoke to the assembled guests and told of what Christ meant to him. They were amazed – so was an agnostic girl who had come to see me, arrived early, and had been brought into the lunch-party. Somehow her list of objections to the Christian faith (which she had prepared to test me with) faded into irrelevance. She had seen something of what Christ can do in bereavement, and it was one of the factors that brought her soon afterwards to faith.

The resurrection of Christ gives a pointer to the future of the world

There is a lot in the Bible about God preparing a new heaven and a new earth, with new people to live in them. It is beautiful and poetic, and we might be inclined to leave it at that, were it not for the resurrection. But in this one person, the new creation has already taken place.

Perhaps God still has a purpose for this world of ours? Perhaps he will take the constituent elements within it and recreate them for something new? At all events the resurrection of the body of Jesus seems to be a sign that God is interested in re-ordering rather than scrapping this universe he has made with such care.

Dr Roger Pilkington, in his book *World Without End*, has offered this interpretation of the resurrection of Jesus. It is worth pondering. 'If matter is no more than an arrangement of energy, then it is perfectly conceivable (if surprising) that where the sheer essence of the whole creation was poured into human form, the body could dissociate into sheer energy and redistil, as it were, outside the tomb, in a state which was, on the average, more energy than matter, but definitely material enough to have some shape and substance.'

Could it be that what took place in Christ at the midpoint of history is a pointer to God's purpose for the new creation, of which Christ is the head, at the end? One day we shall know!

I was very struck recently in seeing how a brilliant philosopher, literary man, and man of action, Jean-Paul Sartre, faced the future of mankind. He was a passionate atheist who in earlier life had written books like *Nausea* and had not flinched from drawing the most fearless consequences from atheism. In 1980 he wrote in a journal on the subject of despair and hope:

With this third world war which might break out one day, with this wretched gathering which our planet now is, despair returns to tempt me. The idea that there is no purpose, only petty personal ends for which we fight! We make little revolutions, but there is no goal for mankind. One cannot think such things. They tempt you incessantly, especially if you are old and think 'Oh well, I'll be dead in five years at the most.' In fact, I think ten, but it might well be five. In any case the world seems ugly, bad, and without hope. There, that's the cry of despair of an old man who will die in despair. But that's exactly what I resist. I know I shall die in hope. But that hope needs a foundation.

It does indeed.

That foundation is the empty grave and living presence of Jesus Christ. You will find it nowhere else.

Alas, within a month Sartre was dead: did he find that foundation which he longed for?

The resurrection needs to find a counterpart in the believer
Before we leave the implications of the resurrection, there is one very important one which Christians tend to ignore. It is that the cross and resurrection of Jesus are intended to find a counterpart in our lives. 'He himself bore our sins in his body on the tree, that we might die to sin and live to righteousness', or 'We were buried . . . with him by baptism into death, so that as Christ was raised from the dead by the glory of the Father, we too might walk in newness of life', or 'always carrying in the body the dying of the Lord Jesus, so that the life of Jesus may also be manifested in our bodies' (1 Peter 2:24; Romans 6:4; 2 Corinthians 4:10).

The point is this. The cross and resurrection are not merely external to us. They must become part of us. There needs to be a real dying to sin and self-centredness in each one of us. And there needs to be a real appropriating of the power and radiance of the resurrection. You cannot have the power of the resurrection without being willing to tread the way of the cross. You cannot have the crown without the thorns. Triumphalism, therefore, has no place in authentic Christianity. There will be triumph, but it will be the triumph of the crucified. The Corinthians wanted the power of the resurrection without going the way of the cross. Paul told them it could not be done: that is why he was determined to 'know nothing among you except Jesus Christ and him crucified' (1 Corinthians 2:2).

Part of the paradox, part of the in-between-ness of being a Christian in this age, is that we are *both* subject to the pain and fallenness of a world that has run amok, *and* are also heirs of the kingdom of God with all its power and glory. Many Christians are unaware of the power that God means them to have, the very power of the resurrection itself. Many Christians who do know that power have forgotten that they cannot escape the self-sacrifice and suffering. As ever, Paul had the balance. His aim was 'that I may know him and the power of his resurrection, and may share his sufferings, becoming like him in his death, that if possible I may attain the resurrection from the dead' (Philippians 3:10ff.).

Those are just some of the implications of the greatest event in history, the resurrection of Jesus Christ from the dead.

6

Assessing the New Age

So far so good, you may think. This has been just a re-presentation of what the Church has always taught, when it has been true to its charter. But if we were to leave it there it would totally neglect one of the major religious forces to have emerged in the past two hundred years. I refer to the New Age Movement, the most modern, comprehensive joyous and eclectic of all attempts at religious syncretism.

1. THE NEW AGE

The background
It is not easy to get a handle on the New Age and its beliefs, because it is profoundly uninterested in dogmas. It is a loosely knit and constantly evolving world view which poses a strong challenge to rational-ism and Christianity alike.

The last thirty years should have prepared us for something of the sort. In the sixties there was a tremen-dous optimism among the young. The counter-culture held out much hope of a new world. It was the day of flower power, with slogans such as 'Make love, not war'. It was the day of the sexual revolution and of the drug culture.

The seventies saw the flowering of the human poten-tial movement, with endless self-help ideologies, expensive seminars designed to enable you to discover yourself, and a good deal of Eastern mysticism as a backdrop.

This trend was continued in the eighties, which coupled a tremendous drive towards material success and wealth with a (paradoxical) reaction against the emptiness of materialism. But what to put in its place? Astrology, the occult, concern for the environment, exploring the feminine principle in the cosmos, acupuncture and hypnotism, fornication therapy and, above all, hedonism. I want to do it *my* way!

All of this prepared the way for the New Age, which embraces many of these themes, and has organized them not into a series of doctrines but at least into a general outlook shared by such groups and submovements as humanistic psychology, new thought, third wave, third force, the new spirituality, the human potential movement, the holistic movement, and a great deal of the environmental caucus. The aim of these thousands of cooperating organizations across the world is nothing short of the formation of a new world order of peace, fulfilment, harmony with nature, fusion with the One, transcendence of human nature to self-divinity. It believes the troubles and miseries around us spring from the simple error of attributing reality to the separate, limited, individual existence which is such a mark of Western man. The remedy for our situation is enlightenment, recognition of the god within us, self-realization. This is possible for any of us who are prepared to step outside the ordinary ways of looking at things into an altered mode of consciousness which dispels the illusions of separate existence and brings us into one. And in the end, this universal union will make an end of individual life in general and our personhood in particular. Death is the supreme liberator, for it ends the alienation of personal existence by ending the existence of the person. At the end, all rivers flow back into the sea.

The world view

It would be rash to attempt to outline the general world view of the New Age, but most New Agers would subscribe to something like this account of their outlook.

The world is not self-existent and Godless, as the materialists have maintained; no, the world itself *is* God, and is worthy of our worship. It is impersonal and amoral, but it is one, spiritual and conscious. We need to get in tune with it.

Human beings, so far from being naked apes, as many humanists maintain, are in fact sleeping gods. They share the divinity of the cosmos, and wait to be awakened to that truth.

Human problems are self-induced, and the remedy for them is to be found within the recesses of our own potential. We neither need, nor can we have, any rescue from beyond ourselves. We do not need it, because there is no basic difference between good and evil. We cannot have it, because there is no power outside the cosmos itself, no personal Creator God. Human problems will yield to human solutions, provided that there is that change of consciousness, that recognition of the divinity within that the New Age so strongly maintains, along with its pantheistic predecessors. Evil is an illusion, induced by ignorance of our true potential. Death, too, is an illusion: it is the gateway to the next life, which is cyclical, going round and round without arriving anywhere. Reincarnation, therefore, is only to be expected. It continues until all individual personhood is erased, and all human beings are sucked up into the universal Unity. All religions, too, point beyond their individual particularities to this universal One from which we all come and to which we all go. Jesus, therefore, is simply one of the many *avatars*, periodic manifestations of the divine. He is certainly not to be worshipped. He is one of us.

The attraction

It is not difficult to see how attractive all this is, derived as it is from Eastern monism allied to Western humanism. It speaks to our desire for one world, one faith, one destiny. It avoids the uncomfortable distinctions between right and wrong, maintaining that they are in the end illusory. It gives some hope of another life after death. It draws together men and women of goodwill from all nations and faiths into a single movement for the preservation of the earth, the banishing of all wars, and the realization of our divinity in the coming Age of Aquarius. It panders to our pride, in teaching that our resources are all within us. It allows us to remain agnostic about any personal source of our world and our lives. It gives us the supreme gratification of supposing that we are gods, and that it is ignorance, not moral failure, which prevents us from attaining our destiny – ignorance which a change of consciousness can transform. It allows us to regard Jesus as just another religious teacher. It advocates the syncretism which is so congenial to the liberal human spirit. It speaks to issues which Christians and materialists alike have been slow to address: the environment, various kinds of oppression and the sterility of the technological society. It offers a spiritual dimension to life after years of barren materialism, but a spiritual dimension which is compatible with a great deal of materialism and hedonism. It is undemanding in lifestyle, liberated from dogma, and immune to the claims of traditional morality. This is a very powerful mix. It is not surprising that it is sweeping great tracts of the Western world.

The essence

It would, of course, be a great mistake to suppose that the New Age is new. It is nothing of the kind. It is a mixture of the Gnosticism that nearly sank the early church, the pantheism into which the soul always returns when it turns its back on a transcendent Creator, and the Eastern monism which has always been very impervious to the Christian faith. Those strands, coupled with the cult of the self, reverence for the cosmos as revealed by science, the recovery of spiritual awareness, and openness to the occult (through channelers, crystals and the like), lie at the heart of this movement which is very hard to characterize because of the diversity of its beliefs and its rejection of rational argument. The New Age believes that the mind, which has been supreme in the age of rationalistic humanism, simply gets in the way of experience. We are not to evaluate, not to judge, not to think. We should simply experience God, become God, and bow the knee to our own divinity. Reason is not competent to judge experience. It is not difficult to see in all this a massive revolt against the barren bondage in which the Enlightenment has for so long held the human spirit. Irrationality, so far from being a vice, is hailed as a virtue.

It is therefore very difficult to dispute with New Agers. The laws of logic will get you nowhere. But the great thing is that experience will. They are very willing to consider religious experience from whatever source it comes. And I believe that the most powerful bridge into the mindset of the New Age, and the most effective way of helping its adherents, is to concentrate attention on the resurrection of Jesus Christ.

2. THE RESURRECTION – A BRIDGE INTO THE NEW AGE

Both reject rationalism

I believe we owe the New Age a great debt of gratitude for having exposed the dominant assumption of Western thought for the past two hundred years: that the mind, reason, is king. In the great centuries of the Christian faith, reason was enormously valued as a God-given faculty of the highest significance: but it was never worshipped. It was subordinate to God and was open to the possibility of his intervention in his world. It was patient of miracle, compatible with spirituality. But when God was dethroned, reason took his seat, and a cold rationalism ensued. Nothing was valued unless it could be measured and tested. Of course, this left no room for the things we most value in life such as love, creativity, beauty and the like. But scientific materialism brought such benefits to us through its technological wizardry that we tolerated its arrogant dogmatism. The theologians followed suit, and a powerless, grey, non-miraculous Christianity emerged which had little power to attract and no power to convert. But the New Age has cried, 'A plague on both your houses'. It has rebelled against the dogma that claims rationality as the bench-mark of humanity: it has gloried in the irrational, in feeling, in celebration, in unfettered exploration of the universe of the spirit as well as that of the material world. The New Age has been an important part of the revolt against the rationalism of the Enlightenment which has brought about what we call post-modernism. And with all this the Christian wants to join hands. For we, too, refuse to believe that the sieve of rationalism will catch the whole of reality. We, too, believe in something profoundly opposed to cold reason: and yet we do so on solid rational grounds. For, as we have seen, though the resurrection of Jesus cannot be proved scientifically, there is in its favour such a mass of evidence that it is very hard to deny. When we show the evidence of the resurrection to the New Ager, we affirm his refusal to be in bondage to rationalism, but we deliver him from the necessity of rebounding into irrationality. It is a wonderful access route into his attitude of mind.

Both celebrate life
Again, there is something wonderfully liberating and joyful about the New Agers. They celebrate life. They revel in their humanity. They have a great sense of

hope in the future. And the Christian says 'Amen' to all that. But we have far better grounds for our joy. It is not based on revolt alone, reaction against a cold rationalism: it is based on the fact that the last enemy has been faced head on, and defeated. It is based on the indisputable fact of Easter. What joy that brings! What hope for the future! There really is a future for *homo sapiens* despite the disasters and follies of the human race. Our hope is based not on the supposed unity of all mankind and the hoped for New Age of Aquarius, but on the fact that the first fruits of the New Age have already emerged from that dark tomb at the first Easter. And in that one seed we see the destiny of the whole crop. The Christian hope of a better future, the Christian hope of ultimate human destiny, is not based on wishful thinking but on solid fact, the resurrection of Jesus Christ from the dead.

Both value the transcendent
There is a third area in which the Christian can come alongside the New Ager. Both value the transcendent. Both believe that reality is a lot larger than what we can see and measure. The New Ager has some grounds for this in elements of human life such as joy, love, creativity and the like. But the Christian has much stronger grounds in the resurrection of Jesus Christ from the dead. That is the supreme demonstration of the transcendent in our world. That is the supreme proof of the beyond breaking into our midst. If the New Ager *values* the transcendent, the resurrection *demonstrates* it.

Both emphasize experience
We have alluded to it already, but I want to salute the New Ager for his or her emphasis on the importance of experience. In this New Agers join hands with their predecessors, the hippies and the Existentialists who refused to be bound by logic and history, and wanted to

assert their humanity through experience, of whatever kind. The Christian is delighted with that attitude. It is very Christian. For we never imagined that we could prove the existence of God: you don't prove personal existence – you meet people! And the living, personal God of whom the Bible speaks is there to be met and enjoyed. Experience, not essays, are the nub of it – though you would never guess as much from the way we train our clergy, still under Enlightenment paradigms of books, credibility, and reason. As every true Christian knows, the heart of the Christian life is relationship with Jesus: the Jesus who died for us on the cross, and is alive to be met and to be the companion of all who will become his disciples. If Christianity is just another religion or ideology you can keep it as far as I am concerned! But it is not. It is a relationship – with the most wonderful person the world has ever seen. And he is alive: he can be met. So often the New Age shares the Existentialist inability to describe or even verbalize the experience that turns them on: 'You have to be willing to have experiences and not have words for them,' wrote Marilyn Ferguson, one of the standard bearers of the New Age. But why so? Why should you not be able at least to point to the source of the experience you have had? That is precisely what the Christian does. He or she revels in the friendship of Christ. It is the most important relationship in life, and it is perfectly possible to talk about it, to explain a good deal of what it is like, and to point to the strong arguments in history and reason for its authenticity. So there is no need to pit reason against experience. Experience is what lights us up, but we do not have to sacrifice our intellectual integrity to discover it.

Both value spirituality
Closely allied to their stress on experience is the New Age emphasis on the importance of spirituality. We do not have to go along with the amorality of their view

of spirituality, nor to embrace its occult and nature-worship overtones, in order to agree with them that spirituality is crucial for humankind. We are, as they realize, made for worship. And if we subdue that instinct it will only find release through the adulation of royalty or pop stars, the Party or the dictator, the car or the GNP. If man is not a worshipper, he is bound to be an idolator. We all need to recognize the spiritual aspect of life. We all need to acknowledge that which is greater than us and draws us by its beauty. It is not difficult for a Christian to come alongside a New Ager in this matter. We both have very similar attitudes, and they are light years away from the cold materialism of Enlightenment man. But can we not go further than our New Age friend? Can we not point to Jesus, risen from the grave, as the supreme example of the triumph of the spiritual over all the physical misfortunes, including death, which befall us? And can we not challenge him to produce any comparable example in the history of the world which better illustrates the triumph of the spiritual? The New Ager values spirituality. The resurrection of Jesus shows it at its most powerful and compelling.

3. THE RESURRECTION – A CHALLENGE TO THE NEW AGE

But having drawn alongside the New Ager and applauded many of his attitudes (while at the same time taking them on a stage further) the Christian will want to look to the resurrection as a decisive refutation of some of the errors in the New Age.

The resurrection challenges syncretism

First, the New Age is syncretistic. All religions lead to God, or at least are husks of which the kernel is one Unity. This is a very attractive doctrine in a world that has been split by religious wars and that desperately needs to find unity. The resurrection, however, gently but firmly affirms that it is not true. All religions do not lead to God. Indeed, none of them do. All are human attempts to reach the divine, however he or it is defined (and to their credit, New Agers are most reluctant to define the divine, lest they limit it). The resurrection of Jesus from the grave is utterly unique. It shows that the one who has been raised is unique. Humanly speaking, as the Epistle to the Romans puts it, he was born of David's stock. But the resurrection set him in a place to which no other has attained. He is powerfully shown to be Son of God. The resurrection sounds the death knell of syncretism. All religions do not point the same way; they do not reach the same goal. The divine is infinite and we are very finite. The divine is holy and we are not. The gap yawning between us is immense. We do not need a religion. We need a revelation and a rescue. And that is just what the resurrection of Jesus offers us. The resurrection underlines those claims of his to bring God into the midst, to make God manifest within the confines of a human life. And the resurrection puts the seal of confirmation on the job he did on the cross, taking personal responsibility for the evils of mankind. The uniqueness of Jesus stands out with startling clarity at the empty tomb. He is not one of the many *avatars*: he is the only. He is not one of the many great teachers: he is the Risen One.

The resurrection challenges the impersonal

Second, the New Age is, in the last analysis, impersonal. All monism is. It maintains that our individuality, our personhood is all part of *maya*, the illusion under which we human beings labour. Its hope for human destiny is very bleak. All it has to offer is reabsorption into the universal One, where all personhood, all individuality is, after many reincarnations, erased. The age-long tension between the One and the many, the personal and the impersonal is resolved. The New Age offers us only the One, and the impersonal. But if the resurrection of Jesus Christ is true, a very different scenario emerges. That resurrection validates the ultimate place of the personal in the universe. Nothing can vanquish the person who is utterly devoted to the will of God: even death cannot hold him down. And the destiny of Jesus foreshadows the destiny of his followers. They will not be rubbed out at death, as the materialists claim. They will not be absorbed in the universal, impersonal One, as the New Agers claim. They will have a personal relationship of love with a personal God and with all others who love him: and that relationship death itself will not be strong enough to break. What a powerful concept: making room as it does both for the survival of the person and for the continuance of love, which instinctively we all feel to be the most wonderful thing in life. Here is a picture of the future which makes sense, is far more attractive than the ultimate extinction and absorption which the New Age offers, and is solidly attested by the resurrection of Jesus Christ from the dead.

The resurrection challenges naturalism

Third, the New Age can see no further than nature, nature for which it has tremendous reverence. That is commendable: worship of *Gaia* is very understandable. But what if there is a God who transcends nature? What if this world is not all there is? What if our personhood is not some biological freak but the deliberate image of the personal God we cannot see but in whose creativity we share? There is no way in which these two rival world views could be settled – unless it were by means of the resurrection. That event, unique in history, validates the claims to deity of the one who rose. That event reveals him as the human embodiment of the Creator God. It shows him as the Omega as well as the Alpha of all history. The physical world leads the New Ager to worship nature. The resurrection of Jesus within this physical world leads the Christian to worship the God of nature. It says to the New Ager, 'Your world view needs enlarging'.

The resurrection challenges self-worship
Fourth, the New Ager hopes to find all his resources within his own person. He seeks the divinity within. Jesus had powerfully contravened that view during his human life. He had maintained that, so far from being divine, we were both finite and sinful. That it was from the deep recesses within the human heart that all evil emerged. That we were neither naked apes nor little angels: we were fallen creatures, capable of great good and of great evil, and that by no means were these two to be equated. Which world view is right? Surely the resurrection gives the answer. It is here that we find the lie given to human self sufficiency. The resurrection makes it very clear that Jesus is divine and that we are not. We are not divine, and we are not able to achieve our potential on our own. We need the strength of the one who lived that perfect life, and died and rose to release the power of his endless life within us. 'Our sufficiency is of God', wrote St Paul. It is the height of arrogance and the acme of folly to believe that we are divine. That is to so devalue the word as to make it meaningless. *Time* magazine, an unlikely source for Christian orthodoxy, came up with a scathing indictment of the New Age in their issue of 7 December 1987, which concluded as follows:

You can see the rise of the New Age as a barometer of the disintegration of American culture. Dostoevsky said that anything is permitted if there is no God. But anything is also permissible if everything is God. There is no way of making any distinction between good and evil. . . . Once you have deified yourself, which is what the New Age is all about, there is no higher absolute. It is a recipe for ethical anarchy, and it is a counterfeit religious claim.

That is precisely what the resurrection underlines.

The resurrection challenges reincarnation

One of the strong tenets of the New Age is belief in reincarnation. This is imported from Hindu thought which sees history as a circle rather than as a line with a clear beginning, mid-point and end – which is the view of Christianity. Reincarnation has nothing to offer us. It is linked with the doctrine of *karma*, that you inevitably reap the consequences of what you have done; if not in this life, then in some future existence. Such a world view has no room for forgiveness. You pay your debts, without any hope of remission. That stands in startling contrast to the good news of Jesus, that he has himself once and for all paid our debts, and he is risen again to assure us of the fact. He was, as St Paul put it, delivered for our offences and raised again because of our acquittal. Wonderful news! As a result, our destiny is not to go through many purgative reincarnations until the grossness of our lives is melted away, but after death to share in the resurrection life of which the Easter Jesus is the pledge. 'To depart is to be with Christ, which is far better.' 'We shall be like him, when we see him as he is.' That is the conviction of those who knew him. Is it beyond belief? Not reincarnation, based on *karma*, but resurrection, based on the cross and resurrection of Jesus, which points both to our forgiveness and to our destiny. A totally different world view. And one which challenges us to make up our minds, and choose.

The resurrection challenges the occult

A sixth area where the Christian must challenge the New Ager is this. The scriptures in both Old and New Testaments are strongly opposed to spiritualism of any kind: and the modern channeller is nothing more than the old medium in new dress. This the New Ager will recognize. But the Bible forbids it. 'There shall not be found among you anyone who practises divination, a soothsayer, a palm reader, a sorcerer or a charmer, a medium or a channeler or one who summons up the spirits of the dead. For whoever does these things is an abomination to the Lord.' Why? Because it represents man's attempts to cross the boundary (which God himself has set) between this world and the next. Such curiosity is frequently harmful and sometimes fatal. But in the resurrection of Jesus we see the reverse of occult speculation and investigation. God comes to show us the first and clearest example of what lies on the other side of death. Through the resurrection of Jesus he assures us that there is indeed a life after death, that his Son has pioneered the way, and that he is well able to take his disciples there after their death. Meanwhile, he holds the Christian dead in his hand. Nothing in all creation can wrest them from him, for he is the risen one, the conqueror of the last enemy, death itself.

The resurrection challenges near-death experiences

New Agers are very interested in relating and hearing about near-death experiences. They claim them as evidence for the reality of the supernatural, and for the transcendence of time and space. Now none of these stories relate to death or what comes after it; merely to what is experienced *very near* death or perhaps after the heart stops and prior to resuscitation. What if someone were actually to come back from after death, and tell the tale? Would that not be of surpassing interest and relevance? Well, somebody has! That is what the resurrection of Jesus proclaims. That is why he has the last word to say on the subject of death and the beyond. That is why he has an authority unparalleled by any other. For who else has broken the chains of death and risen, radiant, from the tomb?

No, the New Age has nothing to offer us. It offers what it cannot deliver. It is whistling in the dark. It is looking back to a threadbare spiritualism while it claims to usher in the Age of Aquarius. And while the resurrection of Jesus has much in common with New Age speculation and aspiration, in the last analysis it has to say a gentle 'No'. For the New Age did not begin in the 1970s but in the 30s of the first century.

When Jesus Christ rose from the dead, the New Age dawned. The age of assured forgiveness, the age of a new spiritual power, the age of a unity which transcends all divison in his family the Church when it allows his Spirit to control it (as it often does not!). His resurrection has ushered in the New Age of confidence about the hereafter, of jubilation in the present, of care for this world while we await the next. Unlike the teaching of the New Age, which is complex and hard to grasp, the resurrection is simple, powerful and very challenging. Far from whistling in the dark it enables its followers to walk in the light. It is very good news. And it is not a new faith, an ideology derived from the various streams which gave it birth, but a real event, unique and unprecedented – by which we date our era. Christ rose from the dead, and will never die again. Death has no more dominion over him. So sang the 'New Agers' of the first century. They knew that a new chapter in cosmic history had dawned. And we may share their confidence.

7

Taking the Plunge

Since the New Age philosophy is an engaging but mis-
leading cul-de-sac, we are forced to make up our minds
about the resurrection of Jesus Christ, the day when,
in a sense, death died; the day when God's New Age
dawned. What are we personally going to do about it?

We get some light on the appropriate response from
a remarkable source, St Paul's address to the Athenians,
recorded in Acts 17.

We are confronted with the most sophisticated back-
cloth in the ancient world: cultured, civilized Athens.
And in the foreground sceptical, cynical *dilettanti* who
'spent their time in nothing except telling or hearing
something new' (verse 21). They belonged to contrast-
ing outlooks on life. The Epicureans were pleasure-
seekers; the Stoics put duty first. And Paul takes them
all on – Paul the traveller, the theologian, but above all
the evangelist, whose 'spirit was provoked within him
as he saw the city given to idolatry'.

What did he have to say to this formidable audience,
when they gave him a full hearing? No fashionable
message. Oh, to be sure, he began where they were,
using the local landscape for a text. As he passed
through the city he noticed an inscription 'to an
unknown God'. The traveller Pausanias, a century later,
records altars at Athens to 'gods both named and
unknown'. So Paul set out to introduce them to the
'unknown God' whom they worshipped but did not

know. He was the God who had made heaven and earth, and had created us with the express purpose that we should seek after him and find him. Mankind has refused to turn to the Creator and has replaced him with various idols. Nevertheless God has overlooked all that. Until Christ came.

> But now he commands all men everywhere to repent, because he has fixed a day on which he will judge the world in righteousness by a man whom he has appointed, and of this he has given assurance to all men by raising him from the dead.
>
> Acts 17:30–31

Could anything be more inappropriate than a message like that before so civilized an audience? All this talk of repentance, judgment and resurrection? Yet that is what Paul did. And he was right. Paul knew the dangers of endless intellectual discussion, of playing with serious issues. So he gives this strong, peremptory challenge. We need to heed it, just as much as they did in first-century Athens.

Take a close look at that remarkable challenge.

Whom does God command to repent? All men. No less. Pleasure-seekers must repent. Conscientious hard-working Stoics must repent – for they too have sinned and fallen short of the standards of a holy God. He offers forgiveness on the grounds of what Jesus did on the cross. But nobody can have that forgiveness until he repents.

Repentance is not a matter of beating the breast and pretending to be very wicked and very contrite. It is a matter of letting go all you know to be wrong and coming to the Lord to ask him to forgive you, accept you, and face you in a new direction. It is absolutely indispensable. Nobody has ever become a member of God's family without it. That is why God does not suggest it or advise it. He commands it. And if it is *God* who commands all men to repent, only a fool would ignore it.

God might very well have left it there. But he did not. He cares too much. So he gave a reason for his command.

Why should we repent? Because he has fixed the day when he will judge mankind, and judge them by the standard of Jesus Christ. That is why it is so important to repent and get right with him.

Can you face the judgment of God with confidence? I can't. My words and actions, my thoughts and attitudes, the wrong things I've done and the good things I haven't done, all crowd in upon me. 'My sins have taken such hold upon me that I am not able to look up', said the psalmist. I feel a bit like that. Not at all confident about facing the perfect justice of a holy God.

And it will be absolutely fair. I will be judged – you will be judged – by no alien standard, but by what it means to be fully alive, fully human. The standard will be man as he ought to be, Jesus. His love will show up our apathy; his unselfishness, our greed; his purity, our lust; his integrity, our deceit. We shall be compared with him.

Need I say what the verdict will be?

That accounts for the urgency of Paul's plea. The gospel is not something to be debated, but to be acted upon. We need to repent, because if we do not there is no hope for us. We shall be judged. And we shall be condemned. Not so much for failing to reach God's high standards, but for being such fools as to reject his remedy.

'Ah', we can almost hear the Athenians saying, 'but who can believe in judgment these days?' Paul had his answer ready. He continued, 'Of this he has given assurance to all men by raising him from the dead.' His argument is very clear. The judgment is as certain as the resurrection. The resurrection, improbable as it might have seemed, took place in the past. The judgment, improbable as it might seem, will take place in the future. Paul argues from a past certainty to a future one. The resurrection is certain; the judgment is certain. And because nobody can evade it, God commands all men everywhere to repent and entrust themselves to the one who can enable them to face it undismayed.

'All men everywhere.' That is very comprehensive. The resurrection is addressed to all men everywhere. It speaks to the uninformed: the man or woman who, like the Athenians, had never looked into this sort of thing before. It presents them with clear evidence that there is a God, that in Jesus Christ he has come to us, has died for our sins, and confronts us as the conqueror of death. The resurrection has always been the clearest evidence for the honest enquirer to grapple with.

The resurrection speaks also to the fearful: the person who knows quite well that the Christian story is true, but can't face up to what it will cost. Jesus, the risen one, comes alongside and says, 'It is I, do not be afraid.' Is it the fear of what friends will say if you change sides? Is it the fear that you will not be able to keep it up? Is it the fear that he will take from you some pleasures you are most reluctant to release, or make impossible demands upon you? He understands those fears. All his first followers had them too, when he met them after the resurrection. They found, and you will find, that there is one force in the world stronger than fear. It is love. 'Perfect love casts out fear', said John, from experience (1 John 4:18). And once you allow his perfect love to touch you, your fear will melt away.

'All men everywhere.' That includes the doubters. God has been very gracious to the doubter. He has provided strong, palpable evidence, through the resurrection of Jesus Christ from the dead. That evidence is more than sufficient to warrant belief. We have examined it together. But it will only become *decisive* for you once you take the plunge of commitment to this Jesus. Then you will not just know about him. You will begin to know him. Many a person has come to Christ full of doubts and hesitations, saying in effect, 'Lord, I believe; help my unbelief', and has found that even so hesitant a faith, provided it is placed in Christ, opens the door to genuine Christian life and assurance.

'All men everywhere.' That includes the apathetic, the person who likes dabbling in religion, or is out for any new experience, provided it does not involve commitment. I am sorry: but you cannot come to Christ like that. He is not a pleasant diversion. He is not an aspect of religious experience. He is the one who rose from the dead. He is the one who will judge mankind – judge even you – at the end. There will be no playing around then. We shall have to live with the decisions we have made and the character that has emerged from those decisions. He commands all men everywhere to repent.

Very well, you say. I believe Christ rose from the dead. I want to get in touch with him, but how do I actually begin?

It is very simple, like most of the really important things in life. If you are in earnest, you can start today. I suggest you get alone, or maybe find a friend who is already a Christian, and get on your knees and pray some prayer such as this:

'Lord Jesus Christ, I believe that you came to this earth for the likes of me. I believe you died on the cross to deal with my alienation from God. I believe you rose from the dead and are alive for evermore. Lord, I have kept you out of my life for too long. I realize it will be costly to follow you. I realize there will be a lot of spring-cleaning for you to do. I am ready for that, so far as I know. Please come and share my life with me. And make good that promise you gave to your first followers, "Lo, I am with you always".'

Or, if you prefer, something even shorter. When Thomas was persuaded that Jesus was alive and was beckoning to him, he simply fell at the feet of the Master and said 'My Lord and my God' (John 20:28). That was as profound an act of commitment as it was possible to make. And Jesus accepted him. He will do the same for you.

Did he not say 'him who comes to me I will not cast out'? Learn that verse. You will need it, because you will assuredly be tempted to doubt in the early days of your discipleship. It comes in John 6:37. Learn it by heart, and when doubt strikes, use that promise to repel it. Or this one: 'This is the testimony, that God gave us eternal life, and this life is in his Son. He who has the Son has life; he who has not the Son of God has not life' (1 John 5:11–12). What a magnificent black-and-white promise to claim!

Maybe you still feel uncertain. Perhaps you fear you might not do it right, or that you do not know enough of him to take that plunge. I wonder if this will help you?

I remember a husband and wife coming to see me during a mission in which I was involved. The wife entrusted her life to Christ, much as I have suggested above. The husband went away to think about it. He returned on the last night of the mission. 'Michael,' he said, 'I haven't got there yet.' He was a really honest person. So I said to him, 'Why don't you pray a simple prayer entrusting as much of yourself as you are aware of to as much of Jesus as you know?' He did so, and almost immediately the joy of making contact with the risen Christ began to fill him. You see, it is not the amount of faith we have which is important, but where that faith is placed. Even slight and doubting faith, if it is put in the risen Jesus, enables his life to begin flowing into ours.

Well, suppose we take that step. What next?

Let us see what the earliest disciples did in order to develop their own knowledge of the risen Jesus. I think they might give us some such advice as this, on the basis of their own experience of Jesus subsequent to Easter day.

Meet the Master

Meet him often. They did, and each time it brought joy and encouragement.

Prayer is the way in which we meet him. Prayer at any moment in the day – brief, informal, natural. Though prayer was probably a last resort before we entrusted our lives to him, it begins to become as normal as breathing to the Christian. The barrier of alienation has gone down. We are in touch now, and it is a growing joy to share experiences with him, just as two friends would on a long walk.

Join the community

Isolated Christians are an anomaly. We need the community and the community needs us. Thomas missed the blessing of Christ's appearance on the first Easter evening because he was not with the others – for what reason we do not know (John 20:24). No wonder the writer to the Hebrews warns us not to neglect to meet together, but to encourage one another (Hebrews 10:25). Even if you feel the church in your area is not very exciting, it is most important to get identified with it. Isolated Christians are easy meat for Satan.

Read the book

The two disciples walking to Emmaus on the first Easter day had a wonderful experience from the stranger whom they later realized was the risen Jesus. 'Beginning with Moses and all the prophets, he interpreted to them in all the scriptures the things concerning himself.' And their response was characteristic of Christians

ever since: 'They said to each other, "Did not our hearts
burn within us while he talked to us on the road, while
he opened to us the scriptures?" ' (Luke 24:27, 32).

Regular reading of the Bible is as important to spiritual growth as regular meals are to physical develop-
ment. If you go short on this you will become a dwarf
– or starve. It is as critical as that. And if you think that
it is all a bit of a chore, you are wrong. The Bible will
become your favourite book because in it you will meet
afresh with Jesus Christ, and your heart too will burn
within you as he opens to you the scriptures, and
makes them come alive.

Eat the meal
It was not only the scriptures that thrilled the hearts of
those two disciples on the road to Emmaus. It was also
the meal with Jesus. 'When he was at table with them,
he took the bread and blessed, and broke it, and gave
it to them. And their eyes were opened and they recog-
nized him' (Luke 24:30–31).

All the way down the centuries Christians of every
tradition and nationality have found the same. He *does*
meet us in the breaking of the bread. He feeds us and
we recognize him as we gather round the Lord's table.
The Holy Communion is one of the main ways of growing in the knowledge of Jesus.

If you mean to develop the relationship, make sure
you attend the meal.

Live the life
As a member of the 'community of the resurrection'
your life will be different from what it used to be. We
come to Jesus just as we are, but he does not leave us
unchanged. He gets to work on us. That is why there
is so much teaching in the epistles of the New Testament on practical Christian behaviour. Not, mark you,
aping the Christians around you. They may have got it
wrong, in part at least. But it is a matter of seeking to

please Christ in all we do. Provided we keep close to
him in the ways already indicated, a lot of this change
will come imperceptibly. The New Testament says that
changed character is not something we work up, but
fruit which the Holy Spirit produces in our lives once
we give him access: 'love, joy, peace, patience, kind-
ness, goodness, faithfulness, gentleness, self-control'
(Galatians 5:22–23). This is fruit that grows in Christian
lives.

Use the power
He has the strength you need for living the Christian
life. You don't. Therefore it is essential that from the
very outset you start turning to Christ and claiming his
power in your temptations, in your moods of
depression, in your loneliness and in your failures.

There is an enemy of souls, as you will very quickly
discover if you haven't already. And his strategy is not
to encourage you to commit terrible sins; it is much
simpler than that. He wants to keep you out of touch
with Jesus Christ. Therefore your prayer life will be
attacked. So will your church-going, so will your Bible
reading. He is out to distance you from Jesus your Lord.
If he can achieve that, he will be well satisfied. So if
you want to make a success of the Christian life, make
sure that you keep close to Christ. For the Christian life
begins when you put your life in the hands of the risen
Lord, and it grows riper every day as you keep your
life in those hands.

Here is a concrete illustration of that transforming
power of Jesus. Fred is a cockney. He was, as he himself
put it, 'an embryo gangster, already with a list of crimes
which society could level against me, and sins which
accuse me of their own accord'. The story of Fred's
conversion (in a big rally which he entered for a dare
to 'meet a bird'!) is fascinating enough, but the sequel
is more interesting still. He became an Army padre.

This is what he has to say about the revolution which has made him the man he is:

> The living Christ has given me what no court, no psychiatrist, no probation officer could give me – the consciousness of sins forgiven. The living Christ has given me a sense that he understands and cares for me, which no other friendship has ever fulfilled. This alone has been of enormous therapeutic value to my scarred soul.
>
> The proof of the pudding is in the eating. The proof of a living Christ lies in a personal relationship with him. My experience of him since my conversion has been varied, and with trials enough to make me very sure of him. Army life, on active service with the Parachute Brigade in various parts of the world, has removed the possibility of my faith being due to weak sentimentality. The harsh reality of fighting the continually exposed weaknesses in my own character (in particular, refusal to acknowledge my limitations, coupled with smugness and self-assertion) has dismissed the possibility of my experience being merely emotional. Emotion does not sustain the continuing effort needed to suppress the passions which war against the soul.
>
> The personal discipline that education and character-training have demanded of me is not likely to have sprung from wishful thinking! The joy of a loving wife, two children and a happy and secure home, have shown me that through the living Christ even one who, like myself, was once described by a magistrate as a 'social menace' can be more than just tolerable. That is something of the difference that Jesus Christ has made, and continues to make to me.

Such is the testimony of one of the most complete men's men it has ever been my privilege to meet: paratrooper, footballer for the Army and Brighton, boxing champion, and so on. All Fred's potential gangster-like characteristics have been taken over, redirected, and harnessed by Jesus Christ. That is what the risen Lord can do in any one of us, once he is invited to take control. What other power is there in the world that can do the same?

Let's end with the three questions with which this book began.

What is life all about? The purpose of life is to know the living Lord and to enjoy him for ever.

What is the supreme need of our society? To be reconciled with the Jesus who died for us and rose again. Once in touch with him, each of us can become what we are meant to be in society: 'light' and 'salt' was how Jesus put it.

Is there a life beyond the grave? Indeed there is, and that has been crystal clear since the new age dawned. Don't miss it.